FIRES

A Guide To Financial, Internal, Relational, External, and Spiritual Transformation

Daniel Purdy

Published by Daring Business Strategies Inc., November 2017
ISBN: 9780999630402

Editor: Kristin van Vloten
Typeset: Greg Salisbury
Book Cover Design: Marla Thompson

DISCLAIMER: Readers of this publication agree that neither Daniel L. Purdy, Sr. nor his publisher will be held responsible or liable for damages that may be alleged as resulting directly or indirectly from the use of this publication. Neither the publisher nor the author can be held accountable for the information provided by, or actions, resulting from, accessing these resources.

In my experience, successful strategic planning, implementation, and execution require dedication, consistency, stability, and adaptation to change. This applies to the corporate environment as well as to the home. Growing up, my mother exemplified these qualities with her positive attitude and loving behaviors. Rearing three rambunctious boys wasn't easy, so she would often muse, tongue in cheek, "I don't mind what you do in life, as long as you're with me in Heaven." Of course, Mom's impactful words and loving example were meant to help align our rather circuitous paths with the straight and narrow. Could that have been my first personal vision statement? I continue to heed her salient advice. This one's for you, Mom.

Acknowledgments

I am very grateful to my project team, who made this book possible. Thank you Kristin Van Vloten, for leading me through the process and for helping me to finally complete this effort. I also appreciate my publishers, Greg and Julie Salisbury, for their enduring patience and attentiveness to every detail for you, the reader.

I'd like to specifically thank the following individuals and families for their remarkable support of my personal and professional development through the years. They each played some role in my own discovery and refinement of the Financial, Internal, Relational, External, and Spiritual (F.I.R.E.S.) personal strategic planning system. Thank you so much: Allison Purdy (and our amazing children); Jerry and Christel Cook; the Dare Family; the Demarco Family; the Eagan/Phillips Family; the Hahn Family; the Jamieson Family; the Koniers Family; the Mentges Family; the Morgan Family; the Piche Family; the Purdy Family; the Righi Family; the Slovarp Family; the Walters Family; the Williams Family; and the Zapotichny Family. I thank God for each of you (and countless others) for your particular influence in my life.

Foreword

Successful leaders say that problems are solved by making decisions; problems are avoided by making good decisions. The one good decision too few of us are making is the one to take ownership of our own potential. The problems that result are formidable—but totally preventable.

My career as an executive coach and leadership researcher has allowed me to work with the business world's best and brightest. My clients have included GE, Microsoft, Pepsi, Novartis, Time-Warner, NASA, American Express, Dell, Kraft Foods, Citicorp, Deloitte, Kellogg's, McDonalds and UAL—to name a few. That has meant diving deeply into powerhouse organizations to discover the humanity that drives them.

I can say that many leaders and team members within these juggernauts epitomize human potential firing on all cylinders. I can also say that some of the people behind the world's most iconic brands are sacrificing some of their greatness in a misguided attempt to be successful or productive.

Daniel Purdy has come up with the key to unlocking this "greatness", this "potential" that some are squandering. He writes, "It's about an individual's cognizance of their own core values, and a systematic approach to letting those values drive every part of their life balance. It's about actively, thoroughly reclaiming the humanity behind the worker, the leader, the community member, and the world citizen." And he's right.

Now, we hear a lot about core values these days. We hear a lot about meaning and purpose. But do we hear about addressing these concerns with strategic planning best practices, with the rigorous methodologies my corporate clients excel in? Do we often pair strategy with soul, planning with purpose? Knowing something and doing something about it are two different things; Daniel helps you to do both.

As it turns out, the people I have worked with who have the tendency to sacrifice their need for a values-driven, balanced existence possess just the tools required to turn their situation around. They know how to plan; they just don't harness those planning skills to address neglected parts of their lives.

As a veteran of corporations just as sizeable as my top clients, Daniel Purdy is well versed in the strategic planning methodologies that boost bottom lines. In fact, if you know Daniel like I do, you'd be likely to describe him as the ultimate, left-brained planning maniac. Nobody enjoys a flowchart quite like he does.

But there's so much more to Daniel than his expertise in supply chain management and corporate vision casting. He's also somebody who chose to walk away from the big salaries and impressive titles to conduct his own personal re-set. He knows what it's like to desperately need a re-think—and to take it.

F.I.R.E.S. is the fruit of that re-think, which took Daniel on a journey from corporate employment to entrepreneurship to coaching. It distills his insights on walking a path that diverges from the cookie-cutter or soul-sacrificing existence too many are choosing. It leverages his deep knowledge—and passion for—strategy to enable you to be more intentional about living your best life, which must thrive in places beyond the boardroom.

I like the way Daniel describes the typical, burnt-out, modern individual as an overworked fire fighter, exhaustedly moving from one destructive inferno to the next. In five distinct but interrelated arenas of our lives—the spiritual, the external (i.e., our broader communities), the relational, the internal (i.e., the personal), and the financial—we feel consumed, ravaged, burned to a crisp. We keep thinking that life—the life we dream of—is on the other side of these continually re-igniting fires.

But the answer isn't on the other side of these fires. It's within them. It comes with learning how to harness the creative power of life's five fires so that they stop behaving destructively. That all starts with the decision to conduct a re-think. Re-think your perception of stress, success, balance, and goals. Then make some hard but worthwhile choices.

When I ask CEOs and C-level executives, "What's the most difficult part of your job?", they almost always respond with: "Responsibility for decisions." However, when I ask them, "What's the best part of your job?" the nearly unanimous response is: "Freedom to make decisions."

Harnessing your potential necessitates living within that paradox. Making decisions means bearing the load of responsibility as well as feeling a singular sense of freedom. Is it easier to live on autopilot, neglecting your soul to just go with the flow, accepting what others are willing to dole out to you? Of course. But is the choice to avoid making choices ever satisfying? Of course not.

Whether you are a seasoned pro or an emerging leader, choose to harness your own potential. It's a decision I promise you won't regret. And most importantly, it's a lesson you'll teach the next generation by example.

Read on!

Debra Benton

President, Benton Management Resources, Inc.

Author, *The Leadership Mind Switch* (McGraw-Hill)

Contents

One

Creation or Destruction?

An introduction to the F.I.R.E.S. personal strategic planning system

The Drones

He was one of those colleagues. We've all had them. If you flip to "corporate drone" in the dictionary, you might just find his picture.

He was inches away from retirement but the light had gone out from his eyes long before his impending freedom put him on autopilot. If you asked him a question it took him hours or even days to respond. He had no discernable enthusiasm to advance any cause more profound than a long lunch break. He was the definition of a clock-puncher, a corporate lemming.

And most horrific of all? For me, he'd become the poster child for walking that long corporate road towards professional apathy. After all, he wasn't the only colleague I knew whose light had been dimmed to the point of being extinguished. With the glass-half-full perspective I had at the time, far too many others seemed to be exactly like him. Half-heartedly sitting through meetings. Avoiding the extra mile like the plague. Being put through their lusterless paces.

Is this what happens to people in this place? I wondered. When I considered this man, my colleague at one of the world's foremost technology companies, I wondered if I was watching my own fate unfold.

It enraged me. It scared me. That's not who I am at all, I thought. I had always believed that work was a privilege, not a right. I took the idea of making a contribution seriously. But could

I become my own version of this man?

I'd floated into this blue chip corporation on a cloud of newly minted achievements and outsized ambitions in the 1990s. I had relocated from a suburb of Philadelphia to Colorado, thrilled to start working as a Procurement Coordinator for a Fortune 100 company. I was firmly committed to changing the world—nothing more, nothing less. I had the brains, the training, and the determination to do gigantic things.

I just knew those gigantic things would be accomplished under the auspices of my iconic new company. After all, it was an organization that, for decades, had been producing the marvels of a nation all fired up to push technology forward. Its story was a beautiful one: the classic tech myth of a few visionaries in a garage who managed to create a world-changing brand. The legacy of this company was sobering, inspiring, and just the right size for developing my own personal legacy within it.

In Pennsylvania, I had a reputation for being an over the top achiever. If there were a high school yearbook category for "Most Likely To Go Beyond", I would have received top billing. I was the guy who didn't just believe in the inspirational calendars—I lived them out, guns blazing. I could never walk slowly or ride my bicycle at a coasting speed. All systems were go; all controls were set for the sun; all phasers were set to stun.

I was the perfect candidate for success in corporate America. Or so I believed.

In many ways, this company proved to be every bit the inspiring entity its origin story suggests. Never a tech guy, I nevertheless learned everything I could about circuits. I observed my engineering colleagues fitting unbelievable numbers of transistors onto 6 millimeter-sized integrated circuits, calling it "black magic" with utmost admiration.

In addition to the drones who disturbed me, I met brilliant, committed people. My supervisor, who taught me everything about procurement and supply chain management, became a dear friend in addition to a professional mentor. And there were plenty of others like her.

I received an education like none other. It was one thing to study business administration in a university. It was another thing entirely to see, from the inside out, how a company that sold hundreds of millions of dollars of product each year operated. I could see for the first time how excellence could be managed throughout an enormous organization, from employees to managers to suppliers to executives.

Plus, my systematic, logical mind thrived on the company's management processes. I learned about quality management systems and lean production techniques. My brain swarmed with ideas for reducing the time it took to produce widgets. I learned to hunt out waste and dispatch with it like a corporate knight.

But in the late nineties, the winds of change were picking up speed, particularly in my sector. Despite my company's sterling history and penchant for managerial excellence, it was operating before a backdrop of increasing volatility. Tech companies were flooded with cash. It was a time of mergers and acquisitions that occurred at breakneck speeds. Companies reorganized, power changed hands, and legacies were interrupted.

In 1999, my company spun off from the iconic brand I'd hitched my professional ambitions onto. Suddenly, I was working under a different masthead. I had gone, along with the furniture, to a new professional home. I was rattled.

Furthermore, the spin-off came at a time when my frustrations were already mounting. In addition to the wearying, water-torture-like effect my more drone-like colleagues had on me, I had recently tasted serious disappointment. I had worked tirelessly on an exciting project that earned me a write up in a tech journal. But the product was ultimately quashed when it wouldn't cash flow.

The go-getter I was (and still am, if I'm honest) was being forced to swallow more bitter pills than I had the stomach for. I had to accept the truth: no matter how enthusiastic and hardworking I was, there were forces at work in corporate America that had no concern for my well-being or self-actualization. The plan I had for my life just was not in alignment with that of those who actually held the purse strings. Plus, the negative mindset I tended to have at that time of my life truly made everything worse. Things were genuinely less than ideal, but in my mind, they were horrendous.

I hated the level of stress all that corporate volatility entailed. In the World War II version of America that had nurtured my dreams, workers chose a company, worked hard, and stayed there until they chose to leave. The thirty-year plan meant something in those days. But I was finding I had a shelf life of about three to five years, when it came down to it. After dealing with pay cuts, cost of living adjustments, and the hard choices that come with taking on new, unexpected roles, I was feeling squeezed to the breaking point. In addition, I would watch upper management types blow whatever money all of this frenetic reorganization generated on cigar collections or fast cars. I made the sacrifices, and the big boys on top frittered away the rewards.

By the year 2001, a millennium was ending but the era of corporate plate tectonics showed no signs of slowing down. And I'd had enough.

I decided, in my infinite wisdom, to take a break from the corporate world to run a Loveland, Colorado based juice bar I'd acquired. Enough technology. Enough widgets. I wanted a small business I could really wrap my arms around and manage exactly the way I wanted to.

Ultimately, I spent five wonderful years at that juice bar. Going out on my own and scratching my entrepreneurial itch was good for me. I employed 15 people and loved working with them. Plus, I gained something special out of the business that I'd never expected. A glorious woman took a job as my General Manager— and eventually I convinced her to take the position of being my wife.

In 2001, getting the juice bar up and running wasn't my only concern. My exit from the corporation had stirred up something inside of me—something fierce, energetic, and undeniable.

Ever since I was a child, I'd had a strong Christian faith. In 2001, my disappointments, worries, and enduring hopes were causing me to re-examine that faith in a whole new way. If my core values meant so much to me, then how could they direct me in this time of uncertainty? How could or should they be driving my decision-making processes, my plans, my ambitions?

What I'd seen in corporate America had sometimes inspired me and sometimes disgusted me. In so many ways, its culture contrasted sharply with the vision espoused by my faith. If corporate America valued the bottom line above all else, my faith valued caring for people above all else. If corporate America stood for greed, my faith stood for generosity. If corporate America taught me to sacrifice my health and happiness to a stressed-out existence, my faith taught me that my body was a temple I should revere.

And yet...there were aspects of what I'd learned working in a multi-billion-dollar corporate environment that legitimately inspired me. What about those? What about the lessons, best practices, and insights of systems and standards like ISO 9001? What about the things I knew about managing excellence and planning for the best possible outcomes?

I wanted to know: How can I take what I've learned about planning and managing excellence and marry it with my deepest beliefs and core values? How can I plan for a life that yields not only material success, but also expresses what matters the most to me?

So in 2001, I started journaling like a madman. It started out as a prayer journal, just me recording the cries of my heart. I wrote out my hopes and dreams. I asked myself what my needs and wants were, and what direction I wanted to go. I was in a deeply spiritual place, overjoyed to have the space to let my soul do some stretching out and breathing deeply.

Before long—around April of that year—the inveterate planner I'd always been started expressing himself loudly on the pages of my journal. Prayers were becoming lists; rambling thoughts gave way to graphs. Something was taking shape before my eyes.

Through writing about what I needed and wanted out of life, I organically produced a list of areas in my life that, put together, created a striking acronym.

F.I.R.E.S.

Financial: I wanted and needed professional/financial security and success

Internal: I wanted and needed a holistically healthy day to day existence

Relational: I wanted and needed good relationships with friends and family

External: I wanted and needed to make social/community contributions

Spiritual: I wanted and needed, above all else, to live out my core values

I believed these five areas of focus overlapped to provide the best lens for viewing my life. These were the areas in which I could plan for and manage excellence on my own terms. And

I knew that everything flowed from S—from the Spiritual. Hence, I realized F.I.R.E.S. was likely a double "backronym". I knew that to plan and execute the life I wanted and needed, I had to start by defining my spiritual purpose, my deepest beliefs, and my core values. And I saw that anybody else who used a process like the one I was creating needed to start with "spirit". They needed to start with their deepest beliefs and core values, regardless of what faith or tradition they were coming from.

Corporate America taught me that money comes first. But I was starting to see that I could invert that logic, while still leveraging the lessons my time in a Fortune 100 environment had taught me. I could combine planning with passion, systems with soul, strategy with spirit. There was more to life than maximizing shareholder wealth.

Before long, I had fleshed out the backronym into a complete planning process that was as thorough as any I'd used for corporate procurement. I had created F.I.R.E.S., a personal strategic planning system that put spirit where it belongs—at the starting point.

And here, at the starting point of this book, it's my pleasure to share this system with you.

Introducing F.I.R.E.S.

Imagine you are standing in the courtyard of a property you own. There are five butane lighters lined up before you, hovering in the air. Atop each lighter is a neat, blue flame, each one burning to a uniform height.

Suddenly, some invisible force hurls each one of these lighters to various locations. Your entire world is soon ablaze. Your home, your community, and your very self are caught in an unbelievable conflagration. You run helplessly around, looking for anything to extinguish this fire. Your life has become devoted to fighting fires. It's all you can do to survive.

This is what life has become for many. If this type of fire symbolizes stress, anxiety, and turbulent feelings of being out of control, all too many of us are ablaze. Our waking hours are devoted to putting out fires. We do this at work, at home, in terms of our mental and physical health, and in our community, without even realizing it. We're stamping out fires deep within ourselves, in the places where we contemplate meaning and purpose.

Now, imagine that this inferno that only a moment ago was consuming your property has died down. All its destructive effects have been miraculously reversed. You're starting from scratch, with the five lighters once again arrayed before you, burning tiny blue flames.

Suppose you walked up to each lighter and, with clear intent, picked them up and began using them to light different fires in your environment.

You use the first lighter to start a controlled burn of the clutter and tangled vegetation that has accumulated around your property.

You use the second lighter to start a fire in a large brick oven in the courtyard.

You use the third lighter to start a fire in the fireplace that warms your home.

You use the fourth lighter to light a lantern that illuminates your home.

You use the fifth lighter to light the torches that surround your property and keep predatory animals away.

Living a life of continually fighting fires is the reality of many. But this above scenario of lighting and managing five types of productive and useful fires is the reality of people who live their lives in balance.

Fire is a powerful concept, isn't it? Shout, "Fire!" and you'll get anybody's attention. Like other elemental forces—say, water or earth—fire can be either profoundly destructive or phenomenally productive and creative. It all depends on whether you have the skills to manage it.

Each of the five items listed in my F.I.R.E.S. backronym is an aspect of your life that is packed with raw power, pure fuel. When we light these fuel sources and tend their fires intentionally, we can reap the benefits. But when these five fires ignite without our governance and grow uncontrollably, we become their victims. These areas of our life then become sources of stress, destruction, crisis, and unproductive problem solving.

Life shouldn't be about fighting fires that threaten to destroy you. Life should be about harnessing fire's potential to serve you.

The Five Fires

Let's revisit the F.I.R.E.S. backronym that outlines the personal strategic planning process that this book will lead you through. Because it is a backronym, we'll start at the end and work our way to the beginning.

1. Spiritual Fire

When you use the first lighter to start an intentional and well-managed fire, you cleanse your vision by clearing away clutter and create the conditions for regeneration in your life. We use the image of a lighter that starts a controlled fire to clear away unproductive vegetation and make your land more fertile. This component of the process is your starting point for creating the life you want and need. It's your foundation.

Spiritual, the first component of the F.I.R.E.S. system, is geared towards:

- defining what matters the most to you (i.e., your core values and beliefs) and what success in this area of your life would look like, so you can create a Personal Definition Strategy

- analyzing your spiritual situation

- envisioning various scenarios in which you try out various approaches to getting to where you want to go spiritually

- evaluating the solution you chose to figure out whether you're on course towards realizing your Personal Definition Strategy

2. External Fire

When you use the second lighter to start a cooking fire in your courtyard, you're able to prepare a large, sustaining meal for your community. We use the image of a cooking fire to represent the contribution you make to your community and/or the world at large.

External, the second component of the F.I.R.E.S. system, is geared towards:

- defining the social contribution you would like to make so that you can create a Social Contribution Strategy

- analyzing your social/community situation

- envisioning various scenarios in which you try out various approaches to getting to where you want to go in terms of making a social contribution

- evaluating the solution you chose to figure out whether you're on course towards realizing your Social Contribution Strategy

3. Relational Fire

When you use the third lighter to start a fire in the fireplace that warms your home, you're able to keep those closest to you warm and nurtured. We use the image of a fire in your home's fireplace to represent the personal contribution you make to family and friends and the measures you take to keep your closest relationships healthy.

Relational, the third component of the F.I.R.E.S. system, is geared towards:

- defining the way you would like to develop your closest relationships so that you can create a Relationship Development Strategy
- analyzing your relational situation
- envisioning various scenarios in which you try out various approaches to getting to where you want to go in terms of developing your relationships
- evaluating the solution you chose to figure out whether you're on course towards realizing your Relationship Development Strategy

4. Internal Fire

When you use the fourth lighter to light the lantern in your home, you're enabling yourself to move confidently around in the places you inhabit every day. We use the image of a lantern in your home to represent the daily choices you make to live a holistically healthy life. These choices allow you to develop into the person you most want to become.

Internal, the third component of the F.I.R.E.S. system, is geared towards:

- defining the way you would like to live your daily life (e.g., hobbies, self care strategies) so that you can create a Personal Development Strategy

- analyzing your personal development situation

- envisioning various scenarios in which you try out various approaches to getting to where you want to go in terms of developing yourself

- evaluating the solution you chose to figure out whether you're on course towards realizing your Personal Development Strategy

5. Financial Fire

When you use the fifth and final lighter to light the torches that surround your home, you're creating a secure space for yourself, in which you can "keep the wolves from the door". We use the image of torches surrounding your home to represent a good professional/financial situation that makes the most of what you have. These torches support and protect all of the good results you want to see in the Spiritual, External, Relational, and Internal spheres of your life.

Financial, the fifth and final component of the F.I.R.E.S. system, is geared towards:

- defining the way you would like to earn your living and manage your financial affairs so that you can create a Professional Development Strategy

- analyzing your professional/financial situation

- envisioning various scenarios in which you try out various approaches to getting to where you want to go in terms of your profession/finances

- evaluating the solution you chose to figure out whether you're on course towards realizing your Professional Development Strategy

The Four-Step Model

As you can see by reviewing each of the F.I.R.E.S. components, this is a systematic planning process. It allows you to leverage the best practices of strategic planning for your personal development. With every component—from the Spiritual to the Financial—you are creating a strategy that you can implement, test, and perfect. And within every component, you are working through a four-step planning process.

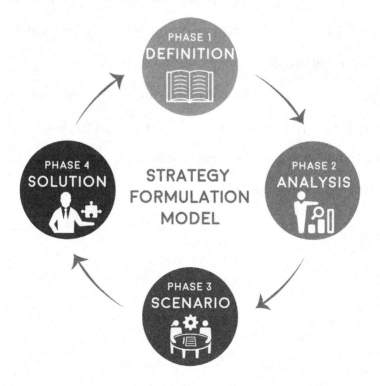

The first step, Defining, involves creating a Problem Statement, or a focused description of the issues, problems, or "room for growth" that exists in a particular area of your life. This step helps you to put a finger on what you're dissatisfied with and start dreaming about what success would look like. The key question here is: "Where do you want to go?"

The second step, Analysis, involves taking a closer look at the past, present, and possible future of your situation as it relates to this particular area of your life. This step allows you to really drill down into where you are, how you got there, and how you might take steps out of the situation you're currently in. The key question here is: "How long will it take to get to where you want to go?"

The third step, Scenario, involves thinking through different solutions, strategies, or approaches for getting to where you want to go. This step helps you to come up with your best possible "answer" for the Problem Statement you created in the Defining step. The key question here is: "How will you get to where you want to go?"

The fourth step, Solution, involves implementing the "answer" you came up with during the Scenario step and testing how well it works. This step helps you to refine your approach, make adjustments, and measure your progress towards your goals. The key question here is: "Did you get to where you wanted to go?"

Key Terms

Here are a few key terms that will surface as you work your way through F.I.R.E.S. Reviewing them in advance will aid your understanding of the process.

Goal

A desired outcome comprised of multiple objectives. Goals should include a barrier or challenge (Hurdle), a measurement component (Index) and a Time component (By when? or For how long?). "H.I.T. the target!"

Objective

A series of well-defined, measurable achievements or milestones that, when executed in succession, ultimately accomplish a goal.

Strategic Initiative

The initial step or series of steps identified in determining or developing a strategy.

Strategic Plan

An important directional document that focuses on the strengths, weaknesses, opportunities and threats (S.W.O.T. Analysis) of an entire organization or an individual. The Strategic Plan answers such questions as: Where are we going? How do we get there? How long will it take? Did we get there?

Strategic Planning Process

The art and science of formulating a high-level plan of action that intricately coordinates information and resources from various sources and disciplines. The major process components include: communication, coordination, identification, research, formulation, documentation, implementation and measurement.

Strategic Priority

The most immediate and crucial requirements or primary desires of an organization or an individual, which are elevated above all other needs and wants.

Strategy

An elaborate and systematic plan of action, intended to accomplish specific goals and objectives. At a minimum, a strategy should include: a problem statement, a situational analysis of time (e.g., past, present and future), consideration of alternative solutions to the problem, and the recommended solution(s) to resolve the initial problem statement.

How To Use This Book

The book that you hold in your hands represents everything you need to work through the F.I.R.E.S. personal strategic planning system. It will guide you through the process of creating and implementing plans for the Spiritual, External, Relational, Internal, and Financial areas of your life. To create each of these five plans, you'll use the four-step model I just introduced you to. As you will soon see, the whole system is laid out, chapter by chapter and step by step, in an easy to follow format.

Essentially, this book will ask you a series of questions, and you can record your answers in whatever fashion works for you. Many people like to use the spaces provided within this book to record their answers, while others prefer to set a journal or electronic document aside for this purpose. Do whatever allows you to feel focused, organized, and inspired.

Throughout this book, you'll also learn a lot about the latest research and thinking around the Spiritual, External, Relational, Internal, and Financial areas of your life. By introducing you to the insights and findings of innovative thinkers, you'll be inspired to dive even deeper into your reflecting and planning. The idea is to give you plenty to mull over as you answer the critical questions that comprise the F.I.R.E.S. personal strategic planning process.

A Word Before Beginning

Before you start working through F.I.R.E.S., remember your purpose in doing so. The idea is to stop fighting life's five interrelated fires, and start harnessing their beneficial properties instead. Shift from mitigating crisis to managing excellence. Turn sources of stress into life-giving resources. This is your opportunity to create structures for living out your core values and having your most essential and meaningful needs and desires met.

I believe we have only about 73.4 years on this planet (or 76 if you're a woman). With that limited time, it's critical to figure out what matters sooner than later. Failure is OK—in fact, it's more than OK; it's necessary. But failing forward is what I'm personally interested in doing. Aren't you?

If my time in corporate America taught me anything, it's that great outcomes can be planned for. You can get what you want out of a systematic, well considered, and thorough approach. You can get to where you want to go with a little defining, analysis, scenario planning, and solutions implementation. These formulas work! Billions of dollars of profit prove it.

But to keep the precious human being inside of these structures alive, inspired, and on-purpose, we need to start with spirit. We need to start with core values and deepest beliefs. When we inherit our "purposes" from machine-like, inhuman, and bottom-line-driven entities, it can kill our souls. It can turn hardworking go-getters into dead-eyed drones.

I didn't want that for myself. And I don't want that for you. Let's start exploring a better way now.

Two

Your Spiritual Fire

Cleanse your vision, clear away clutter, and create
conditions for regeneration

The Haven

Authentic community wrapped around a spiritual core. That's how Dr. Matthew Gamble, my brother-in-law and the pastor of a Californian church, describes his core value. It's his True North, the ideal that steers his decision-making at all levels of his life. It's the core value that inspired him and his wife Susan to turn their lives upside down, ushering in what has truly been the best of times—and the worst of times.

Five years ago, the two of them had been living in a place they considered paradise: Florida. Matthew had started a non-profit organization for which he'd been traveling globally for five years. Susan had just finished her residency as a doctor at Yale University. Together, they had just welcomed their first child and were raising her in a beautiful home just one mile away from a popular beach.

Their life in the Sunshine State was, as Matthew puts it, "storybook perfect", but there was one catch. Susan and Matthew were not connected to community, not really. They both came from a faith tradition that was extraordinarily meaningful to them. Where they were, there was simply no spiritual community in which they felt comfortable or understood.

If you know Matthew like I know Matthew, that's a big problem. Matthew is a passionate networker and communicator, and nothing stokes his inner fire like connecting with people. He lives to make contact, win trust, and build meaningful community. Isolation and Matthew are not a good mix, not at all.

One day, a solution to the Gambles' paradisiacal yet lonely situation arrived in the form of two simultaneous job offers. One was for Susan at a hospital. The other was for Matthew at a small church. Incredibly, both positions were located in the very same Napa Valley community, thousands of miles away.

Initially, when they traveled to California for their interviews, the Gambles weren't taken with the place. Florida's lush natural beauty had captured their hearts. They had family and friends where they were. Plus, the cost of living in California was daunting. Were these jobs worth the dislocation and the lifestyle changes?

But once they returned home to Florida, Matthew took a walk on the beach to pray and suddenly the decision seemed clear. A door was opening for him and Susan. Something bigger than his qualms was drawing him to Napa Valley, where the church he was being asked to lead was on the verge of being shuttered. That church's leadership felt he could inject their spiritual community with desperately needed new life. Matthew felt ready to find out if that was true.

Authentic community wrapped around a spiritual core was calling him.

So the Gambles went to California. And what unfolded was, according to Matthew, "the hardest season of [his] life by far."

The church was nestled in a small community with fewer than 1,000 people. The hospital where Susan began working was adjacent to the church, built by the same church pioneers over one hundred years ago. And what the Gambles represented was a modern, and for some, unsettlingly radical approach to that faith's tradition.

"Culturally, what I stand for rubs some people the wrong way," explains Matthew. "For others it's very refreshing, inviting, and redeeming. But I've never faced personal persecution like I have living here. I'm a threat to certain people."

In pursuit of authentic community wrapped around a spiritual core, Matthew has helped to revitalize a previously dying church, which became, under his leadership, simply known as "The Haven". With his 21st century approach to a legacy denomination, many left his building. Still more began attending, and formed vital smaller groups within it. The church is now nurturing pockets of true friendship that are living out the vision of community Matthew has long dreamed about. The Haven lives up to its name; it's now a judgment-free zone where people are safe to share and explore.

But the flipside of that church's revitalization was Matthew's marginalization in the broader community. He has been the target of painful vitriol and gossip. "It's been an absolute firestorm," he says.

Part of this firestorm entailed what Matthew refers to as a nervous breakdown that forced him to go on administrative leave. He was having heart palpitations, couldn't sleep, eat, or breathe right, and much of the time he "wanted to be vaporized".

Despite all that, Matthew sees the past four and a half years of his life as some of his best. They have been "extremely refining and very life-giving."

The firestorm of judgment he experienced in Napa Valley—so acutely painful for an individual who delights in winning people over—has acted as a refining fire. The pain has teased out, and then started to ameliorate, particular character flaws. It drove personal demons out of hiding. Matthew describes the way a goldsmith knows he has burned the impurities out of gold when he or she can see his or her reflection clearly in it. Napa

Valley—and Matthew's pursuit of authentic community wrapped around a spiritual core—has shown Matthew his own reflection.

Matthew knows that certain people in the community continue to speak negatively about him. Although it feels like a punch to the gut, it also shows him how far he has come. Four years ago any negative comment would have consumed him, echoing in his heart for days, leaving him deflated. Today, he can stand up to the stings and barbs because he knows his community at The Haven sees him differently.

Matthew is actively involved in Recovery circles, which teach freedom from addictions through working the famous "twelve steps". Central to the Recovery movement is a belief in a Higher Power, or a "power greater than ourselves" that can help us when we can't help ourselves. And he believes that the night he walked on the beach in Florida and decided to accept the job in Napa Valley, it was because his Higher Power was leading him.

Matthew believes his Higher Power wanted him to help create a place of safety—a place of authentic community— for the very people now rejecting him in Napa Valley. And in that process, Matthew has shown himself what it means to need a place of safety. Above all else, walking through the firestorm that resulted from pursuing authentic community has shown Matthew what his core value truly means.

"The way I see it," he says, "if there was going to be someone at the helm of a place called The Haven, they had better know what a haven is all about, and what it's needed for. And I do now and I always will."

Spiritual Fire

I opened this chapter with Matthew's story because it's a relevant example of Spiritual Fire's refining nature. Now, you may not personally subscribe to a particular religion, but all people are driven by their deepest beliefs and core values. Governments around the world rise and fall on the strengths and weaknesses of their underpinning constitutions, charters, or articles. For-profit and non-profit businesses likewise need vision, mission, core values, and belief systems to develop strategies and successfully implement their action plans. Matthew's story is simply a great illustration of what that looks like when applied to real people.

When you have clarity around, and fidelity towards, your beliefs and values, you will walk courageously in the direction of expressing them. What happens when you do that is a process of refinement, when the unnecessary is stripped away, and true purpose is uncovered. This process can be extraordinarily elating or profoundly difficult—and in most cases, it's a blend of the two—but it will always involve refinement, focusing, and clarity.

I used to work in an oil refinery in northwest Washington State. Although that amazing chemical process still feels like black magic to me, certain technical truths really stood out. In short, the inbound oil was not going to change itself. It required significant heat, pressure, and catalytic and chemical applications to change and re-form its molecular structure. Only then could we create even more valuable outbound products, ranging from gasoline to calcined coke.

Similarly, the Spiritual Fire that kick-starts the F.I.R.E.S. personal strategic planning system is concerned with identifying your atomic-level core values and deepest beliefs. It's the natural starting point for building a life of authentic joy, driven by purpose and mission.

Like my brother-in-law, Matthew, you are about to identify your True North, the values that will refine your character and narrow your strategic vision. While I hope the trials he has endured in Napa Valley aren't part of your path, I do hope you experience even a fraction of the clarity he has since gained.

Matthew knows what's essential to him. He knows what's worth fighting for. And that means that his worst of times are also his best of times. Wouldn't you like to say the same of yourself?

In this chapter, you will launch your personal strategic planning process, beginning with Spiritual Fire. You'll be reading stories that illustrate the nature and purpose of this Fire. You'll be introduced to a few thinkers that deal with the concept of core values and beliefs. Hopefully, this will stir your own thinking and prepare you to dive deeper into your own planning process. Finally, you'll work through the Spiritual Fire component of the F.I.R.E.S. personal strategic planning system.

At that stage, you will be:

- defining what matters the most to you (i.e., your core values and beliefs), and what success in this area of your life would look like, so you can create a Personal Definition Strategy

- analyzing your spiritual situation

- envisioning various scenarios in which you try out various approaches to getting to where you want to go spiritually

- evaluating the solution you chose to figure out whether you're on course towards realizing your Personal Definition Strategy

That's what's ahead. Let's get started by taking a closer look at the Spiritual Fire and how it factors into creating a vision and a plan for the life you truly want to lead.

Why the Spiritual Comes First

In the F.I.R.E.S. backronym, the Spiritual comes first. But why?

Let's revisit the metaphor of the lighters and two styles of fire (i.e., out of control infernos and well managed blazes) we explored in the first chapter. As you'll recall, I asked you to imagine standing in the courtyard of a property you own. You pictured five different lighters causing a destructive, undifferentiated wildfire that began consuming your property and the community around you. Next, you pictured using these lighters to, with clear intention, start lighting well-managed and productive fires in various sites around your property. And the first fire you lit was for a controlled burn of the clutter and tangled vegetation that has accumulated all around you.

This is your Spiritual Fire. It cleanses, clears away clutter, and creates the conditions for regeneration. In healthy, diversified ecologies, fires occasionally sweep through to burn dense vegetation, freeing up energy for new and different plants to grow. When you have clarity around your core values and beliefs, you can actively wield their power to refine, refocus, and regenerate. You can periodically cleanse the "landscapes" in your life that are storing up too much unproductive vegetation and clutter.

Like Matthew's goldsmith, you will be using Spiritual Fire to burn away impurities until you can clearly see your own reflection.

Lighting and tending the Spiritual Fire is a matter of sweeping away everything that's unnecessary and figuring out what's most essential. Imagine you lit this controlled fire of cleansing and you're now surveying your land. What's still standing? What has the potential to grow in all of that soil you freed up and fertilized with ash?

We need to start with the Spiritual, with defining and making room for our core values and deepest beliefs. We need to do this because without taking this first step, we'll never generate visions and goals that truly represent our "healthiest ecologies". Instead, we'll just add more tangle, clutter, and tinder to the landscapes in our lives.

I own several management consulting companies focused in different areas of business optimization. One such acquisition involves lean training, consulting, and implementation. In short, my teams of lean professionals go into factories, production areas, offices, and various other workplaces to evaluate client operations and then eliminate their wastes. Although process waste and inefficiencies come in several forms, it can only be measured and addressed once it's been identified. We can then improve the process or production line by changing paradigms, re-focusing efforts, removing complexities, and sustaining the new improvements. It involves getting back to basics and focusing on what matters most.

The F.I.R.E.S. system involves creating five plans for creating the life you want to live. But without knowing what matters the most to you, how can you even really know what that life would, could, or should look like? Without lighting and tending your Spiritual Fire, you're at a high risk of setting goals and making plans that simply create more clutter. Instead, you want to ensure that all of your goals and plans align with your core values and deepest beliefs. Without this alignment, nothing you accomplish will really feel like it hits the mark. Trust me.

The Spiritual Fire component of the F.I.R.E.S. system you'll soon work through will help you to better understand your purpose in life. You will create a written statement of vision and mission for yourself. You will further fine-tune and document your "core values and belief system", which will serve as a foundation and a baseline for a Personal Definition Strategy.

Core Values and Deepest Beliefs

Words like "spirituality", "values", and "beliefs" can be vague at best and misleading at worst. To be clear, in the context of F.I.R.E.S., the term "spiritual" need not have religious or even metaphysical connotations. When I use the word "spiritual", I am merely referring to a person's core values and deepest beliefs, which could, for some individuals, be rooted in entirely scientific or materialist schools of thought.

So let's take a moment to define "core values" and "deepest beliefs".

Core values are:

1. The principles that guide your actions
2. Guidelines that clarify what is "right" and "wrong"
3. The way we express our chosen characters or identities; that is, the means by which we actualize our "true selves" or "desired selves"

Deepest beliefs are:

1. Assumptions or convictions that are held as true even when there is no or little evidence to support or prove them

2. A set of assumptions underlying a way of looking at the world or mentally organizing your reality

If you think about it, your core values flow organically from your deepest beliefs. Matthew's core value of "authentic community wrapped around a spiritual core" is very much related to his religious convictions, which are influenced by the Recovery movement. If your core values dictate the way you behave (or at least would like to behave), your deepest beliefs determine what those core beliefs should be. Where does your sense of right and wrong come from? How do you know how to behave, what decisions to make, and what matters the most to you? Why do you want to live one type of life and not another—and what does that say about what you assume to be true? What's your worldview, or your "subjective representation of external reality", in the words of the futurist Alvin Toffler?

Toffler once described a person's worldview as being like a giant filing cabinet. It contains a folder for every item of information coming our way. It organizes our knowledge by providing a grid for making sense of our daily lives. This filing cabinet resides in the deep infrastructure of our minds. Our cultures, families, educations, histories, and a whole host of other factors have had a hand in creating it. Our worldviews allow us to simply live, rather than painstakingly deliberate over every decision. Because it makes life easier and more automatic, it's natural to simply go about your life without becoming consciously aware of what our worldviews look like, how they function, and where they came from.

Having a worldview is like having a heart that beats or lungs that breathe. We take its functions for granted, even as it enables our very existence.

That's why your core values and deepest beliefs can—and frequently do—go unexamined. You're likely to have a whole raft of assumptions that guide your actions from day to day that you are mostly or even totally unaware of. But since these things end up steering the course of your life, it's essential to identify and understand them. Your (examined or unexamined) matrix of beliefs and values propels your actions, and those actions lead to outcomes. In the end, those outcomes become the substance of your purpose, the sum total of your impact on the world.

Beliefs ⇨ Values ⇨ Actions ⇨ Purpose

By understanding the role of your core values and deepest beliefs, and then clearly articulating them, you are setting a course for fulfilling a purpose. Whatever you think your impact on this world should be—whatever you think your purpose is—it all begins with beliefs and values. So when I use the word "spirituality", that's what I'm talking about: a core values and belief system that will drive you towards fulfilling a purpose. That's what your spirituality is.

When you achieve clarity and a sense of intentionality around that core values and belief system, you will have lit and begun to tend your Spiritual Fire. That Fire will always burn away the unnecessary—that which conflicts with or crowds out your values and beliefs—and will open up space for what you should truly be cultivating. The Spiritual Fire creates fertile conditions for realizing your purpose.

What should that purpose be?

The author and marketing consultant Simon Sinek has coined a famous phrase that addresses this need to clarify purpose, values, and beliefs: "Start with WHY". In his book, *Start With Why: How Great Leaders Inspire Everyone to Take Action* , he says:

There are only two ways to influence human behavior: you can manipulate it or you can inspire it.

Very few people or companies can clearly articulate WHY they do WHAT they do. By WHY I mean your purpose, cause or belief - WHY does your company exist? WHY do you get out of bed every morning? And WHY should anyone care?

People don't buy WHAT you do, they buy WHY you do it.

Sinek originally intended this message for marketing professionals, as perhaps you can tell. But I'd argue it has applicability to a wide array of people, including those about to set off on their F.I.R.E.S. journey. When Sinek talks about "manipulating" or "inspiring" people, he is referring to consumers who may or may not buy particular products. But what if you focused this idea—namely, that behavior can be manipulated or inspired—on yourself and your personal journey?

Are you trying to manipulate yourself into doing certain things? Or are you inspired to do them? When you come up with goals for your personal or professional life, do you feel fired up, impassioned, attracted, and motivated? Or do these goals become whips that you use to cajole or control yourself?

We start with the Spiritual because that's where your personal WHY resides. If you think about everything else in this F.I.R.E.S. personal strategic planning system as being concerned with your WHATs, Spiritual is all about your WHY.

Sinek says that people don't buy WHAT you do, but WHY you do it. And I'd say that if you create plans for your life that only concern themselves with those WHATs (e.g., the type of job, relationship, possessions, etc., that you want), in the end, you won't "buy" it. In other words, you either won't fully invest yourself in those plans, or you won't really value their outcomes. If you want to "buy" what you're setting out to do, start with WHY. Start with your core values and deepest beliefs.

Walking Through Fires

Before you transition into contemplating and writing about your WHY—your core values and belief system—I will share a little about mine.

Early on in my career, I joined a business with another group of people. This was an exciting venture, as I'd already experienced working for a couple of Fortune 500 companies, and I loved the idea of growing something from scratch. However, after a while, I started to understand that my business partners and I had similar values but distinctly different beliefs.

As mentioned, core values represent the principles and mores that guide your decision-making process and actions. These are the codes, laws, behaviors or ethics so important to you that you would fight to the end defending them.

Beliefs are your current perspectives, opinions, and conclusions based upon your cumulative knowledge and understanding today. As such, your beliefs are likely to evolve or even change over time.

Many people believe (or disbelieve) in religion, in a Higher Power, in science, in a certain political party, in certain societal norms, in cultural rituals, et cetera. As we become more knowledgeable through study and life experience, our beliefs can also change. The thing is, if our belief system is somewhat undefined or even callow in its development, we simply won't live up to our own purported values. You can readily see this in people's inconsistent actions, poor decision-making, and bad behaviors.

It was this resulting imbalance of values to beliefs within myself—and between me and my business associates—that would eventually lead to our business separation. This experience was devastating, but also clarifying.

Because my faith is important to me, I internalized Scripture during that challenging time. Specifically, I think of Isaiah 43:2:

> When you pass through the waters, I will be with you; and when you pass through the rivers, they will not sweep over you. When you walk through the fire, you will not be burned; the flames will not set you ablaze.

When I think about commitment to integrity and honesty, I think about the sacrifices one makes to remain truthful. We lie because it gives us an advantage. When we are committed to the truth, we sometimes face rivers of opposition and fires of discouragement. But the reward for this commitment is profound—for me, it represents reliance upon and communion with God, or as Matthew would put it, my Higher Power.

I will stress, one more time, that a system of core values and deepest beliefs need not involve particular religious faiths. Just because Matthew and I happen to operate from a basis of religious faith doesn't mean that you will. But we all have faith in something. We all, in our own ways, take leaps of faith that inform our decisions.

Are you ready to take a leap into enhanced clarity around your core values and deepest beliefs? Let's get started with your personal strategic planning process by lighting and tending your Spiritual Fire.

Your Spiritual Fire Workbook

Your Spiritual Fire Process

Before getting started on the Spiritual Fire component of your personal strategic planning process, recall that the entire F.I.R.E.S. system looks like this:

F.I.R.E.S.

Financial: You want and need professional/financial security and success

Internal: You want and need a holistically healthy day to day existence

Relational: You want and need good relationships with friends and family

External: You want and need to make social/community contributions

Spiritual: You want and need, above all else, to live out your core values

We are starting with your Spiritual Fire because your core values and deepest beliefs must steer all other aspects of your life, including the other ones listed in the F.I.R.E.S. system. The work you will do for the remainder of this chapter will culminate in the creation of a Personal Definition Strategy.

As you'll see, this section (Your Spiritual Fire Process) is stylized like a workbook so you can use its pages to record your thoughts and create your Personal Definition Strategy. But if you find the spaces allotted aren't large enough for your notes, please use another document to record your process. This could be a notebook, a computer document, or the walls of your bedroom—just use what makes you feel comfortable and allows you to stay organized.

Ready to start?

Chapter Two

Your Problem Statement

1. Briefly describe the purpose or purposes towards which most of your efforts in life seem to be currently devoted. This could involve your work, your personal life, your relationships, and so on—just think about what you seem to be investing the lion's share of your energy into these days.

2. Briefly describe the first things that come to mind when you contemplate the purpose or purposes you feel drawn to fulfilling. Don't overthink it. Just write.

3. List any behaviors, patterns, or circumstances in your life that seem to be out of alignment with the purposes you'd like to be devoting your energy to. What rubs you the wrong way, makes you feel out of step, or arouses negative feelings?

4. Summarize your previous answers into a brief sentence or paragraph. Identify any purpose-related challenges or gaps in your life that you wish to overcome. This is your Spiritual Fires Problem Statement.

Your Vision Statement

1. It is now 5 years in the future. What have you accomplished in terms of your Spiritual Fires? What continues to excite you? What amazing spiritual transformation occurred over the last 5 years?

2. You are now attending your own funeral. What is the best eulogy or life story that someone could present about you? What do you want the mourners to miss most about you?

3. Summarize your previous answers into a brief sentence or paragraph. Consider how your vision of the future addresses your Spiritual Fires Problem Statement. Identify anything that encourages you to leap out of bed each morning. This is your Spiritual Fires Vision Statement.

Your Mission Statement

1. How would you describe the purpose or mission that your Vision Statement seems to point towards?

2. Briefly list a few actions or endeavors that would concretely fulfill this sense of purpose or mission.

3. Refer back to your Problem Statement and Vision Statement. What specific things must you do now to light and tend your Spiritual Fire?

4. Summarize your previous answers into a brief, action-oriented sentence or paragraph. This is your Spiritual Fires Mission Statement.

Your Values and Beliefs

A. Your values guide your judgment and help you to distinguish between right and wrong. Ignoring or discarding your personal value system would violate your conscience and perhaps cause you to feel guilt. A few common values are honesty, integrity, and respect. List or define the top 10 values you would rigorously protect and preserve.

B. Beliefs are your current perspectives, opinions, and conclusions based upon your cumulative knowledge and understanding. As such, your core beliefs are likely to evolve or even change over time. The most common beliefs consider religion, politics, economy, social behavior, etc. From purely a Spiritual Fires perspective however, list or define your top 10 beliefs.

Chapter Two

Goals and Objectives

This section of the Spiritual Fire Process is truly the moment when you can take your first lighter and create a controlled blaze that will reveal your deepest beliefs, core values, and true purpose.

You now have an opportunity to contemplate which goals you wish to accomplish in the Spiritual Fires portion of F.I.R.E.S.

In this section, you will be using a model for goal-setting that involves identifying hurdles or challenges, figuring how you will measure your progress, and determining any timelines or deadlines for realizing these goals.

Now, turn the page and define your goals for lighting and tending your Spiritual Fire.

Set Your Goals

To set your goals, remember that you need to define your barriers, your index (way of measuring success), and your timeframe.

Spiritual

An example of a Spiritual goal is:

My goal is to overcome my tendency to spend energy judging people (barrier) by spending 75% less time on social media (index: a metric and a measure), by the end of the summer (timeframe).

Briefly write up to 3 goals within the model framework above and then transfer your answers to the next page. On the following page, complete the assignment by writing the 3 necessary steps required (i.e., objectives) to successfully accomplish each goal.

Goal #1

My goal is to: by: by the end of:

Goal #2

My goal is to: by: by the end of:

Goal #3

My goal is to: by: by the end of:

Set Your Objectives

1. My goal is to   by   within

1.1. Objective   1.2. Objective   1.3. Objective

2. My goal is to   by   within

2.1. Objective   2.2. Objective   2.3. Objective

3. My goal is to   by   within

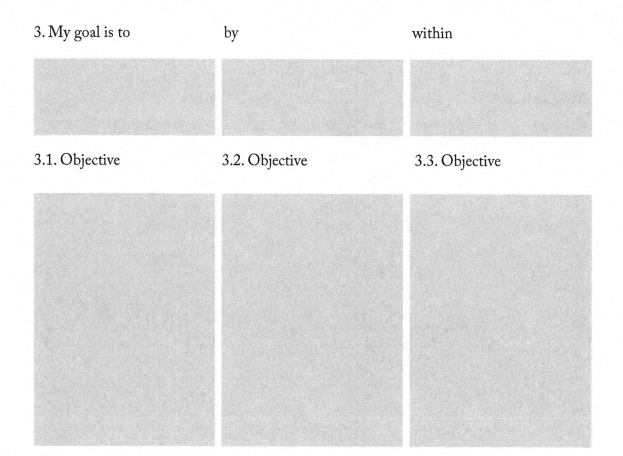

3.1. Objective   3.2. Objective   3.3. Objective

Chapter Two

Your Situational Analysis

1. Transfer your previous Spiritual Fires Problem Statement here. Feel free to tweak or adjust the statement, if necessary.

2. Consider your Problem Statement. What is your history and present standing with this issue? Write a brief paragraph describing these successes and failures. Provide perspective, background, and insight on where you are coming from.

Your Weaknesses and Strengths

List the 5 main strengths you have that can be used to light and tend your Spiritual Fire.

1.

2.

3.

4.

5.

List the 5 main weaknesses you have that may present challenges as you light and tend your Spiritual Fire.

1.

2.

3.

4.

5.

Your Boundaries

When formulating a strategy, there are sometimes boundaries on or limitations to the quality and quantity of alternatives you can feasibly implement.

In the space below, list or describe any resource constraints, prohibitions, concerns or guidelines that might limit your continued formulation of a strategy to light and tend your Spiritual Fires. This may include time, money, desire, motivation, strengths, weaknesses, opportunities and threats.

The Scenario Phase

Congratulations on progressing to Phase Three... the Scenario Phase! All of the Spiritual Fire work you completed up to this point is critically important. Your previous statements and activities will now guide you through brainstorming the possible alternatives and solutions to achieving your desired results.

Problems + Solutions
Goal One

My Spiritual Fires Problem Statement is:

1 . My goal is to   by   within

1.1. Objective   1.2. Objective   1.3. Objective

Brainstorm possible solutions to your Problem Statement or alternative ways to accomplish your goals here. Circle your best options after you have finished.

Problems + Solutions
Goal Two

My Spiritual Fires Problem Statement is:

2. My goal is to   by   within

2.1. Objective   2.2. Objective   2.3. Objective

Brainstorm possible solutions to your Problem Statement or alternative ways to accomplish your goals here. Circle your best options after you have finished.

Problems + Solutions
Goal Three

My Spiritual Fires Problem Statement is:

3. My goal is to   by   within

3.1. Objective   3.2. Objective   3.3. Objective

Brainstorm possible solutions to your Problem Statement or alternative ways to accomplish your goals here. Circle your best options after you have finished.

Think and Reason

Review the possible solutions and alternatives you circled over the last few pages. Why did you choose those circled items and not others to achieve your goals and objectives?

Accountability

How will you remain personally accountable to resolving your Spiritual Fires Problem Statement and to achieving each goal and objective?

How will you track progress and measure your results? What system of organization or other methodology will you use to collect data and manage improvements?

To ensure a successful completion of your goals and objectives, you will need feedback and focus. Choose an "Accountability Partner" to whom you will regularly communicate progress. This can be a relative, a friend, or another trusted person. We recommend someone (other than your spouse) who will keep your best interests in mind.

Accountability Partner: _____

Accountability Partner: _____

Enough talk...implement!

The following page is a summary sheet of the key statements, goals, and solutions necessary to accomplish your Personal Definition Strategy. Tape a copy of this summary to your bathroom mirror, your refrigerator, or wherever else you need to be reminded of your personal commitment.

Return to this Spiritual Fires section in a few weeks after your strategy implementation, to re-evaluate your progress and success.

Enough talk... implement!

Personal Definition Strategy

Problem Statement

Vision Statement

Mission Statement

Problem Solutions

Strategy start date: _____

Strategy end date:_____

Accountability Partner:_____

Accountability Partner:_____

1. My goal is to   by   within

1.1. Objective   1.2. Objective   1.3. Objective

2. My goal is to   by   within

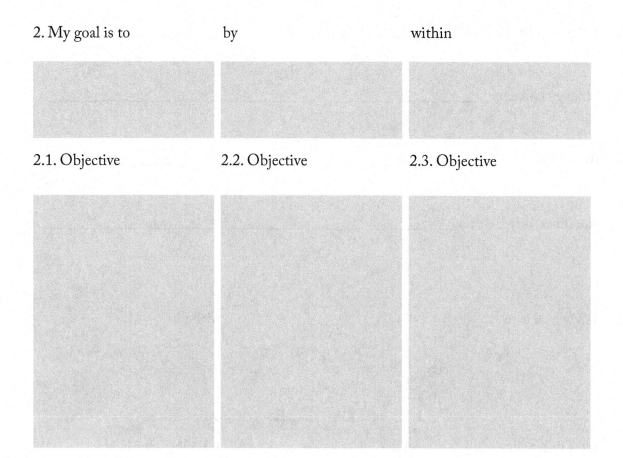

2.1. Objective   2.2. Objective   2.3. Objective

3. My goal is to   by   within

3.1. Objective   3.2. Objective   3.3. Objective

Re-evaluation

1. Now that several weeks have passed since you implemented your Personal Definition Strategy, briefly describe your success in resolving your Spiritual Fires Problem Statement. Are you celebrating each accomplishment?

2. Refer back to the Spiritual Fires Vision Statement you wrote describing your desired picture of the future. Is the "future" you are now experiencing anything like you expected back then? Why or why not?

3. What tweaks or changes must you make to your Personal Definition Strategy? Are you on track to resolve your original Spiritual Fires Problem Statement and related goals? Is it time to repeat these process steps to resolve a new Spiritual Fires Problem Statement?

Spiritual Fire: Core Messages

Your Spiritual Fire is your system of core beliefs and deepest values.

When you choose to actively light and tend a well-managed Spiritual Fire, you experience a clearing away of the unnecessary and enhanced clarity around what is essential. Spiritual Fire is, above all else, refining and regenerating.

Spiritual Fire kick-starts the F.I.R.E.S. personal strategic planning process because clarity around your core values and deepest beliefs will help you make better, more meaningful choices in the other areas of your life.

Three

Your External Fire

Preparing the meal to feed your community

Rainy Days and Rusted Buses

How many rainy days in a row have you experienced in your lifetime? I'm not sure what my own personal record is, but I'll tell you one thing: that number got a lot bigger for me once I moved to the Pacific Northwest.

In 2010, a job with one of the world's biggest oil and gas companies drew me to the bleeding edge of northwest Washington State. If you know anything about the weather in this part of the world, you'll know that terms like "rainforest", "rain shadow", and "rain catchment" are very relevant. Are you sensing a theme?

Having lived previously in Colorado and Arizona (300 days of sunshine per year, anybody?), my family and I found the grey skies and chronic dampness trying, to say the least. It made the loneliness of relocating to a new city that much harder. I mean, the weather itself wasn't exactly warmly inviting us to kick back and feel at home.

We weren't sure if we could take it. My wife and I had several discussions about leaving and even investigated returning to Colorado. Maybe the rainforest just wasn't our natural habitat.

But then, one day, we had a fortuitous conversation with some friends. They encouraged us to spend a little more time in British Columbia, the Canadian province that abutted our town. It was nice, they said, and there were a lot of good schools we might consider sending our kids to. We might as well take advantage of living so close to the border.

So we did exactly that. Across the border, we discovered, among other things, a private school we wanted our kids to attend. We felt this school had a lot of potential. Its culture and engaging learning environment excited us. This was a place that inspired and enabled kids to become amazing citizens and community members.

But the school had one major problem: a boatload of debt. The aged school buses were only one indicator of the strain the institution was under; the oldest vehicle had nearly 680,000 kilometers on it. (That's 422,532 miles, American readers!)

The school was at a turning point, with new leadership who wanted to re-cast a vision for the immediate future. I felt I could help with that. I joined the Board of Directors and rolled up my sleeves.

Our strategic process involved collaboration, teamwork, and a holistic approach to change. I asked open-ended questions of the appointed Strategic Planning Subcommittee. Where are we going? How do we get there? What does success look like? Did we make it? (Sound familiar?) We identified strategic areas of focus, including marketing, management, and operations; and we rebalanced the student aid formula to get those badly needed new buses.

Before this, my wife and I were already invested in our three kids' education, both financially and emotionally. Challenging and purposeful learning had always been of paramount importance to us. But by helping the school to improve, we gained an entirely new sense of meaning from their educational experience. We partnered with dedicated administrators, teachers, and staff to raise the level of quality of each child's education. And it felt so good to buy the first two new school buses and send those dangerously old ones to the junkyard.

After helping facilitate a process that improved upon its vision, mission, core values and beliefs, I know the school can do an even better job of producing knowledgeable and well-rounded students. I feel I did my best for each student who goes through the system—including my own.

Furthermore, something else accompanied those old school buses to the junkyard: our distaste for where we had ended up living. The more my wife and I invested ourselves into community, the happier we became. Nowadays, we're so glad we didn't give up and leave. The school was just a jumping off point for finding a whole network of people and institutions within which we could give and receive support.

I guess when it rains, it pours.

External Fire

What does it mean to you to prepare a meal for your community?

How big a table do you need to set? What kind of food are you serving and how long will it take you to prepare it? What sort of faces will you see assembled around the table?

Within the F.I.R.E.S. personal strategic planning system, External Fire involves defining the contribution you want to make to community at any scale. It's about taking that clarity you developed around your core values and deepest beliefs and doing something about it, starting with the world outside your door.

Now to be clear, when I say "community", I'm not talking about your nearest and dearest.

(Technically, your family members and closest friends do constitute a type of community, according to the dictionary definition. But we'll get to these relationships in Relational Fire.) In the context of F.I.R.E.S., your community extends beyond this core group of people. How far? Well, that's up to you to determine.

For example, the "community" or "society" you invest into could be your township. It could involve town hall meetings, committee groups, or planning sessions with your municipal government. Your banquet table could be set for people around your town who are impacted by issues such as street planning and waste management.

Or the "community" or "society" you invest into could be a group of people in your city, nation, or world who have a common struggle. Perhaps you empathize with the burdens that mothers around the world carry. Your investment could involve joining a charity, holding fundraisers, or brainstorming how to educate people about what mothers endure in particular parts of the world. Your banquet table is set for women from all parts of the world who toast you for making their lives more prosperous, dignified, and safe.

Or the "community" or "society" you invest into could be humanity itself. Perhaps you are concerned with an issue that touches all people in some way. Let's say you became involved in efforts to respond to climate change. You could be educating yourself on the impact of climate change in different parts of the world. You could be writing letters to all levels of government. You could align yourself with charities, advocacy groups, and even business ventures that brainstorm and implement solutions. Your banquet table is incredibly large and set up for huge numbers of people to walk up to, take food from, and leave. You may not formally meet many of the people who enjoy what you have provided, but you'll know it sustained them.

When my family and I moved to Washington, I found a foothold into serving community through my kids' school. The meal I ended up preparing was for a well-defined group of local people: the teachers, administrators, students, and families connected to one school. The meal I served was one I was well equipped to prepare: a strategic planning process that helped this group of people to meet important, measurable goals.

My hope for you, as you work your way through this chapter, is that you will find a community to serve. You have your own version of a "school" that could help you to be more at home in your own life. Find community—at any scale that makes sense to you— and figure out how to make a contribution to it, and you'll never regret it. I know that by doing so, you could radically increase your capacity for contentment and experience of abundance.

Soon enough, you will continue the personal strategic planning process you started with Spiritual Fire. As with Spiritual Fire, you'll read stories and consider ideas that will stir your imagination and fire up your mind. At the end of this chapter, you'll work through the External Fire component of the F.I.R.E.S. personal strategic planning system.

At that stage, you will be:

- defining the community contribution you want to make and what success in this area of your life would look like, so you can create a Social Contribution Strategy

- analyzing your community contribution situation

- envisioning various scenarios in which you try out various approaches to getting to where you want to go in terms of making a community contribution

- evaluating the solution you chose to figure out whether you're on course towards realizing your Social Contribution Strategy

We'll get there soon enough. First, let's dive into the nature of the External Fire and its significance for a successful and meaningful life.

Why The External Fire Comes Second

External Fire calls for an outward focus on serving your community at any scale. Notice that the entire F.I.R.E.S. process involves a seemingly backwards approach to personal fulfillment and self-improvement. If you remain dedicated to this program, it will work like this:

1) Focus on your big picture purposes

2) Express that purpose outwardly in terms of how you care for others

3) Express that purpose inwardly in terms of how you care for yourself

It's not lost on me that this progression flies in the face of current thinking, which tends to recommend self-care first, and social contribution second. We've all heard the metaphor of the oxygen mask on the flight, right? When flight attendants give you the safety rundown, they tell you to use your oxygen mask before helping anybody else to put theirs on. The idea is that if you can't breathe properly yourself, you won't have the wherewithal to save anybody else.

That seems to make a lot of sense. So why don't we move from defining our core values and deepest beliefs right to determining how to best care for ourselves and reach personal goals (Internal Fire)? Once we are aligned with our purpose, shouldn't we be focusing on making ourselves as holistically healthy as possible? Don't we want to be in "good shape" before taking on the world's problems?

Why exactly does External Fire follow Spiritual Fire?

Well, before I explain, let me offer up one caveat. There may be some of you reading this book who have, in fact, neglected their own self-care to a point where this issue deserves your immediate attention. If you know your mental or physical health is truly suffering, don't launch ambitious social contribution strategies before addressing it. In particular, if you are someone who uses "social involvement", "charity", or "community work" to avoid taking care of yourself, proceed cautiously.

You really might need to put your oxygen mask on before fussing with anybody else's.

However, many others reading this will not have pressing health or self-care problems, but will rather suffer from a case of chronic blah-ness. For you, life just doesn't have any electricity, punch, or sizzle. It doesn't have any of the right-down-to-your-bones emotional resonance you imagine truly happy people experience.

For you folks, the answer may not be in focusing on yourself and your myriad dissatisfactions. The answer may be outward. It may be time to test your long-range vision.

In our metaphor of the lighters and two styles of fire (i.e., out of control infernos and well managed blazes) we pictured the External Fire occupying a large brick oven in the courtyard. You use this fire to cook a large meal that can sustain your community—community as you define it, at whichever scale you like. It could be your neighborhood, it could be your city, it could be your nation, or it could be humanity itself.

I would argue that for the vast majority of us, when we prepare a meal for community, we find that we ourselves become nourished. That's why External Fire, above all the other Fires, is about abundance. It's about the miraculous way that sharing seems to multiply rather than diminish our resources. Think of the tale of Jesus feeding the multitudes with five loaves of bread and two fish. In that story, because the bread is broken up into pieces and shared, it miraculously stretches far enough to feed thousands of people. When we give abundantly—when we commit to sharing the resources we have— it has the effect of bringing greater abundance into our own lives.

That's why External Fire comes before the other Fires. When you have cultivated true abundance in your life by serving community, you find your self-focused, short-range, and immediate needs are easier to define and fulfill. If you do the work of lighting and tending your External Fire, by the time you get to your Financial Fire, you might find your needs and wants in that arena simply aren't as consuming. They will have greater focus and will seem more reasonable and attainable. You'll feel good about the reasons why you want or need certain financial outcomes.

The fact is that we deeply need to contribute meaningfully to communities. We need to be part of "something bigger than ourselves" to truly thrive as individuals. And there are certain spiritual, psychological, and philosophical itches many of us never scratch because we don't pursue opportunities to give freely.

In the words of Jean Vanier, the Catholic philosopher and founder of the L'Arche group of communities for individuals with developmental disabilities:

> Individualistic material progress and the desire to gain prestige by coming out on top have taken over from the sense of fellowship, compassion and community. Now people live more or less on their own in a small house, jealously guarding their goods and planning to acquire more, with a notice on the gate that says, 'Beware of the Dog.'

Being entombed in our own homes, jealously guarding the little money, talent, time, or resources we have, is corrosive to our souls, because it encourages isolation. Not being part of anything bigger than your own survival is a lonely way to live. And it turns out that this type of loneliness creates its own vicious cycle.

John Cacciopo, director of the University of Chicago's Center for Cognitive and Social Neuroscience, has studied loneliness for decades. He knows that as human beings, we evolved as "social animals", or beings that can't survive or thrive except in the context of our highly interconnected "tribe". Throughout history, a feeling of being "bonded" to people correlated with good survival outcomes; it meant you were making a valuable contribution to others and could enjoy access to their support when you needed it. However, when a person was evicted from their tribe for one misdeed or another, that person suffered from loneliness, a feeling of social isolation.

That's why, to this day, when someone experiences loneliness long enough, their brain goes into what Cacciopo calls "self-preservation mode". Their visual cortex is enhanced and the part of their brain that is responsible for empathy is weakened. Furthermore, the person whose brain has gone into self-preservation mode has a reduced inclination to seek out the support of a community. That's because, in the past, people who were ostracized from their communities and attempted to force their way back into the group tended to face even more hostility—sometimes even injury or death. It was wiser to just avoid those groups. So, sadly, loneliness tends to create even more loneliness, because in chronic doses it weakens a person's instinct to seek out community.

So are you someone who feels blah, out of sorts, vaguely dissatisfied, stuck, worried, or fearfully hell-bent on protecting "the little" you feel you have? I wonder…could your problem be the terrible loneliness that comes with living in some degree of "self preservation mode"? And is that loneliness creating its own vicious cycle of making you even less likely to look beyond yourself for solutions?

On the other hand, do you feel connected, alive, secure, and as though you have access to all the abundance you'd ever need? I wonder, could this baseline of satisfaction you experience be in any way related to your secure place within a community or multiple communities? Do you meaningfully contribute to society and feel as though you can, in turn, draw upon communal resources (everything from finances to emotional support) when you need them? Do your feelings of abundance and connection create their own virtuous cycles of investing into, and drawing from, community?

Loneliness is inspired by scarcity and produces more scarcity. Connectedness is inspired by abundance and produces more abundance.

That's why External Fire—and not the Fires that focus more narrowly on you or your immediate nearest and dearest—follows Spiritual Fire. It is truly the next logical step. Whether you realize or not, your very brain is designed to be "part of something bigger than you". When you have this connection to community (once again, at any scale), you have access to a natural feeling of abundance. When abundance—a force diametrically opposed to loneliness—is fully operational in your life, you'll find your concerns around self-care, finances, and relationships become a little less intense.

It's not just that your community or your society needs your contribution. It's that you profoundly need to give it. Otherwise, you'll continue to feel as though you are living in the cold, with only yourself to turn to. You'll feel as though you're always struggling to get your own oxygen mask on, perpetually out of breath, stuck in a lonely moment that always feels like an impending disaster.

Chapter Three

Leaders of Giving

In fact, when we look at the connection between abundance and giving back, there are many notable examples showing us the way. Why do you think many of our leaders in business are also our leaders in philanthropy and social change? Many of them know a thing or two about how to creatively generate abundance—and not just for themselves.

Long before he was known as one of the world's leading philanthropists, Bill Gates was famously the world's richest man, the first of an ever-growing line of tech billionaires. He made a fortune through Microsoft, and then co-founded the Bill and Melinda Gates Foundation in the year 2000. The mission of the Foundation was (and is) to fund smart initiatives that improve health, education, and economic development in mainly developing countries. As of 2013, the Gates family had donated $28 billion to the Foundation.

The Gates Foundation just might be the epitome of strategic generosity. You see, the Foundation is notable for more than just its largesse. Its approach to philanthropy involves identifying problems and their most strategic solutions, and setting long-term goals. The Foundation wants to see measurable results from their giving, and they are tremendously invested into the process of seeing those results. In short, Gates runs his Foundation much like he ran Microsoft. He and Melinda are truly in the "business" of tackling the world's most troubling problems, which range from malaria control to agricultural policy.

So far, the Foundation's strategic, intensive approach has yielded a few major success stories. For example, in 2014, India announced it was polio-free, thanks in large part to the Foundation's work alongside the Indian government and Rotary International. They employed two million vaccinators who swept through the country that, five years earlier, had contained over half the world's polio cases. Now the Foundation aims to wipe polio off the face of the planet by the year 2018.

The Gates set a large banquet table—and the meal they serve is always carefully planned.

I can think of another leader in giving who demonstrates the qualities of creativity, strategic thinking, and goal orientation that the Gates have in spades: my friend, the architect Sean Hegstad. Now, the banquet table Sean sets tends towards a more localized community than the one Bill and Melinda are trying to serve. But the meal he dishes out is carefully planned, and always hits the spot.

Sean worked through F.I.R.E.S. with me a few years ago and when it came to External Fire, he had great ideas and a real appetite for giving. After he created his Social Contribution Strategy, he became involved with one of the coolest initiatives I've ever heard of. He works with a group of individuals and businesses who pool their professional skills to do extreme home repairs. They select people in real need—single mothers, people with serious health issues—and help them get their homes into great shape, working for two weeks on each project.

Recently, Sean told me about one woman the group worked with a few years ago. Her house was in total disrepair: rot, mold, water pouring down the side of a wall, and termite damage. She had major health problems and little to no support. In her long list of things to take care of, home maintenance kept getting bumped to the end.

The interesting thing about this woman is that she is a major giver. "She'd help a lot of other people before she'd help herself," says Sean.

The home repairs helped this woman tremendously. Finally, all the giving that she was doing was redirected her way. The repairs reversed conditions that were taxing her already compromised health, and one of the businesses involved in the project actually ended up employing her.

Sean loved being able to invest his skills as an architect into making such a big difference—especially for someone like this woman, a person who would surely take that investment and pay it forward. Sean knows that he's working within virtuous cycles of community and generosity.

"You really feel your own value when you provide something like that to someone else," he says.

Exactly.

Your External Fire Workbook

Your External Fire Process

It is time for the second leg of your journey to personal life mastery. Now that you know how to write a strong and comprehensive strategy, we will begin to move a bit more quickly.

You began this process by proactively lighting and tending your Spiritual Fire with a Personal Definition Strategy. Now that you better understand your core values and your belief system, you can readily apply them to your community (the External Fire).

Before getting started on the External Fire component of your personal strategic planning process, recall that the entire F.I.R.E.S. system looks like this:

F.I.R.E.S.

Financial:	You want and need professional/financial security and success
Internal:	You want and need a holistically healthy day to day existence
Relational:	You want and need good relationships with friends and family
External:	You want and need to make social/community contributions
Spiritual:	You want and need, above all else, to live out your core values

We move from the Spiritual Fire to the External Fire because once you are clear on your system of beliefs and values and the purposes they connect to, it's time to figure out how to express them within your community. The work you will do for the remainder of this chapter will culminate in the creation of a Social Contribution Strategy.

To reach that point, remember that you will be working through this strategy formulation model:

Once again, this section (Your External Fire Process) is stylized in workbook form so that you can use its pages to record your thoughts and create your Social Contribution Strategy. But if you find the spaces allotted aren't large enough for your notes, please use another document to record your process. Just use what makes you feel comfortable and allows you to stay organized.

Let's get started.

Chapter Three

Your Problem Statement

1. Briefly describe your community involvement or the social contributions you make. This could include volunteering time in the local government, hospital, church, library, etc. Include any charitable work or support you provide to others regularly.

2. Briefly describe the degree of community service or involvement you'd like to have. Are you donating too much time and money or not enough?

3. List any behaviors, patterns, or circumstances in your life that seem to be out of alignment with the social or community contributions you'd like to be making. What feels contradictory or undermining to your social values?

4. Summarize your previous answers into a brief sentence or paragraph. Identify any community or social contribution-related challenges or gaps in your life that you wish to overcome. This is your External Fire Problem Statement.

Your Vision Statement

1. It is now 5 years in the future. What have you accomplished in terms of your External Fires? What continues to lead you to serve others? What amazing transformation occurred in you in the last 5 years?

2. You are the guest of honor at an awards dinner and ceremony. What is written on the trophy, plaque, or certificate that caused others to notice and recognize your selfless social contributions?

3. Summarize your previous answers into a brief sentence or paragraph. Consider how your vision of the future addresses your External Fires Problem
Statement. Identify anything that encourages you to leap out of bed each morning. This is your External Fires Vision Statement.

Your Mission Statement

1. How would you describe the community-related purpose or mission that your Vision Statement seems to point towards?

2. Briefly list a few actions or endeavors that would concretely fulfill this sense of purpose or mission.

3. Refer back to your Problem Statement and Vision Statement. What specific things must you do now to light your External Fire?

4. Summarize your previous answers into a brief, action-oriented sentence or paragraph. This is your External Fire Mission Statement.

Your Values and Beliefs

A. Refer back to your Personal Definition Strategy under the Spiritual Fires section. Are there any values that are absent from that list that you now require to accomplish a Social Contribution Strategy? If not, simply transfer those values in the spaces below.

B. Beliefs are your current perspectives, opinions, and conclusions based upon your cumulative knowledge and understanding. Refer back to your Personal Definition Strategy under the Spiritual Fires section. Are there any beliefs that are absent from that list that you now require to accomplish a Social Contribution Strategy? If not, simply transfer those values in spaces below.

Goals and Objectives

This section of the External Fire Process is truly the moment when you can take your second lighter and create a cooking fire that will allow you to prepare a meal for your community at any scale.

You now have an opportunity to contemplate which goals you wish to accomplish in the External Fires portion of F.I.R.E.S.

In this section, you will be using a model for goal-setting that involves identifying hurdles or challenges, figuring how you will measure your progress, and determining any timelines or deadlines for realizing these goals.

Now, turn the page and define your goals for lighting and tending your External Fire.

Set Your Goals

To set your goals, remember that you need to define your barriers, your index (way of measuring success), and your timeframe.

External

An example of an External goal is:

My goal is to help overcome the problem of homelessness in my town (barrier) by volunteering 2 hours a week at a low-barrier housing charity (index: a metric and a measure), by the end of the month (timeframe).

Briefly write up to 3 goals within the model framework above and then transfer your answers to the next page. On the following page, complete the assignment by writing the 3 necessary steps required (i.e., objectives) to successfully accomplish each goal.

Goal #1

My goal is to: by: by the end of:

Goal #2

My goal is to: by: by the end of:

Goal #3

My goal is to: by: by the end of:

Set Your Objectives

1. My goal is to   by   within

1.1. Objective   1.2. Objective   1.3. Objective

2. My goal is to   by   within

2.1. Objective   2.2. Objective   2.3. Objective

3. My goal is to   by   within

3.1. Objective   3.2. Objective   3.3. Objective

Chapter Three

Your Situational Analysis

1. Transfer your previous Spiritual Fires Problem Statement here. Feel free to tweak or adjust the statement, if necessary.

2. Consider your Problem Statement. What is your history and present standing with this issue? Write a brief paragraph describing these successes and failures. Provide perspective, background, and insight on where you are coming from.

Your Weaknesses and Strengths

List the 5 main strengths you have that can be used to light and tend your External Fire.

1.

2.

3.

4.

5.

List the 5 main weaknesses you have that may present challenges as you light and tend your External Fire.

1.

2.

3.

4.

5.

Your Boundaries

When formulating a strategy, there are sometimes boundaries on or limitations to the quality and quantity of alternatives you can feasibly implement.

In the space below, list or describe any resource constraints, prohibitions, concerns or guidelines that might limit your continued formulation of a strategy to light and tend your External Fires. This may include time, money, desire, motivation, strengths, weaknesses, opportunities and threats.

The Scenario Phase

Congratulations on progressing to Phase Three... the Scenario Phase! All of the Spiritual Fire work you completed up to this point is critically important. Your previous statements and activities will now guide you through brainstorming the possible alternatives and solutions to achieving your desired results.

Problems + Solutions
Goal One

My External Fires Problem Statement is:

1 . My goal is to   by   within

1.1. Objective   1.2. Objective   1.3. Objective

Brainstorm possible solutions to your Problem Statement or alternative ways to accomplish your goals here. Circle your best options after you have finished.

Problems + Solutions
Goal Two

My External Fires Problem Statement is:

2. My goal is to   by   within

2.1. Objective   2.2. Objective   2.3. Objective

Brainstorm possible solutions to your Problem Statement or alternative ways to accomplish your goals here. Circle your best options after you have finished.

Problems + Solutions
Goal Three

My External Fires Problem Statement is:

3. My goal is to   by   within

3.1. Objective   3.2. Objective   3.3. Objective

Brainstorm possible solutions to your Problem Statement or alternative ways to accomplish your goals here. Circle your best options after you have finished.

Chapter Three

Think and Reason

Review the possible solutions and alternatives you circled over the last few pages. Why did you choose those circled items and not others to achieve your goals and objectives?

Accountability

How will you remain personally accountable to resolving your External Fires Problem Statement and to achieving each goal and objective?

How will you track progress and measure your results? What system of organization or other methodology will you use to collect data and manage improvements?

To ensure a successful completion of your goals and objectives, you will need feedback and focus. Choose an "Accountability Partner" to whom you will regularly communicate progress. This can be a relative, a friend, or another trusted person. We recommend someone (other than your spouse) who will keep your best interests in mind.

Accountability Partner: _____

Accountability Partner: _____

Chapter Three

Enough talk...implement!

The following page is a summary sheet of the key statements, goals, and solutions necessary to accomplish your Personal Development Strategy. Tape a copy of this summary to your bathroom mirror, your refrigerator, or wherever else you need to be reminded of your personal commitment.

Return to this Internal Fires section in a few weeks after your strategy implementation, to re-evaluate your progress and success.

Enough talk... implement!

Social Contribution Strategy

Problem Statement

Vision Statement

Mission Statement

Problem Solutions

Strategy start date: _____

Strategy end date: _____

Accountability Partner: _____

Accountability Partner: _____

1. My goal is to   by   within

1.1. Objective   1.2. Objective   1.3. Objective

2. My goal is to   by   within

2.1. Objective   2.2. Objective   2.3. Objective

3. My goal is to   by   within

3.1. Objective   3.2. Objective   3.3. Objective

Re-evaluation

1. Now that several weeks have passed since you implemented your Personal Definition Strategy, briefly describe your success in resolving your External Fires Problem Statement. Are you celebrating each accomplishment?

2. Refer back to the External Fires Vision Statement you wrote describing your desired picture of the future. Is the "future" you are now experiencing anything like you expected back then? Why or why not?

3. What tweaks or changes must you make to your Social Contribution Strategy? Are you on track to resolve your original External Fires Problem Statement and related goals? Is it time to repeat these process steps to resolve a new External Fires Problem Statement?

External Fire: Core Messages

Your External Fire is whatever you use to make a contribution to community at any scale.

When you choose to actively light and tend a well-managed External Fire, you create virtuous cycles of connectedness and community. External Fire is about, above all else, abundance.

External Fire follows Spiritual Fire because investing into, and being able to draw from, community will put the rest of your needs into perspective. When your External Fire is lit and preparing that communal food, you are operating from a baseline of abundance.

Four

Your Relational Fire

Warming the place where you live

Two Mad Dogs

When my friend Amy tells me what her dream relationship looks like, she describes the one she's in right now.

"Fundamentally, he's accepting. He celebrates the person I am and gives me plenty of room to do my thing. The last thing he would want to do is control me."

That's a big deal for Amy, because she knows exactly what the opposite kind of relationship is like.

When Amy met her now ex-husband, she was young—in her early twenties—but even then she exhibited the qualities that make her a strikingly unique person today. She had a tendency to express herself freely, sometimes with fiery opinions, sometimes with childlike humor. She always seemed self-possessed, a person who knew her own mind and felt confident in her abilities.

Amy married a young man who she regarded as the smartest person she'd ever met. Their relationship was fun and freewheeling, full of adventures and debates. Her husband seemed to enjoy her company more than anybody else ever had. But relatively early on, there were signs of trouble.

Amy's husband didn't really like her spending time with people other than himself. He also showed a tendency to conceal information or even to tell lies when the truth might cause Amy to take actions he didn't want her to take. Sometimes, when they had conflict, he reacted in ways that disturbed or deeply wounded her. He hurled acidic insults, assumed physically intimidating postures, led her down disorienting verbal mazes, or engaged in long periods of silent treatment.

All of these behaviors eventually caused Amy to shut down. Her submission to his tirades seemed to be the only way she could stop the overwhelming and intimidating stimuli flowing from him to her. She would accept his conclusions or change her plans to suit his whims.

But that wasn't all.

A few years after Amy was married, she took a job at a large company where she was quickly singled out as the ideal assistant for a hardworking executive. She and the executive seemed to get along like gangbusters. He liked her penchant for "telling it like it was" (or at least as she was fairly certain it was). And although she wasn't thrilled to play the ultra-feminine hostess role that an assistant often is expected to assume, she enjoyed discussing strategy with her boss.

The company gave her a cellphone so that her boss could contact her whenever he needed to. And slowly but surely, those times of "need" began to increase. He began to phone and text her at all hours of the day. Now, that's hardly an unusual arrangement for executives and their assistants, but the rules in this situation weren't as typical.

Amy's boss once told her that he hated the very word "boundaries"—and during the years that she worked for him, he proved that he meant it.

He told Amy that under no circumstances was she allowed to turn off her phone. If she was going somewhere without cellphone reception, she needed to clear it ahead of time with him and explain where she was going and what she was doing. He insisted that he would become anxious and stressed if he were not able to reach her at any time or receive a speedy response from her.

Amy had to answer all texts and calls with relative immediacy. If she didn't, she would suffer anxious and angry reactions from her boss. This usually entailed a multiple-hour-long torturous discussion that was similar to the sort she was having with her husband. Amy's boss simply needed her to be always available to him, whether it was for a work-related task or for a therapeutic conversation to soothe his anxiety.

It was easier to be controlled by her boss via her phone than to endure more brow-beatings than she absolutely had to. Eventually, Amy learned to always pick the path of least resistance. She learned to grit her teeth and keep her thoughts and feelings to herself. Above all, she learned to comply as often as she could with the unreasonable expectations being made.

Today, when Amy reflects on her twenties—the decade she was married and worked as an assistant—she describes herself during those years as a woman tethered to two mad dogs.

"Each hand was attached to a different leash and a different dog," she says. "They pulled me everywhere I went, and often in completely different directions. My life was about trying to keep myself together while being pulled apart by two insistently controlling and needy men."

That's a dire situation for anybody. But here's the thing about Amy: one of her core values is freedom. In her F.I.R.E.S. notes, you'll read:

Briefly describe the first things that come to mind when you contemplate the purpose or purposes you feel drawn to fulfilling. Don't overthink it. Just write.

I believe in creating the conditions for others and myself that support maximum freedom. I agree with Nelson Mandela when he said, "the sun never set on so glorious a human achievement" as freedom. I am drawn to living a life that is as independent as possible, and I want to support causes that allow others to live with self-determination and self-expression, free from oppression and fear.

For Amy, living under conditions of unreasonable control, oppression, and fear was antithetical to her core values, values she had accepted at a young age. As you can imagine, the life she led in her twenties didn't allow for much intentional tending to her Spiritual Fire. Every day meant walking through an inferno that felt devoid of meaning or purpose.

All of that changed when she reached age thirty. Her marriage ended under terribly challenging circumstances. A couple of years later, she summoned up the courage to quit her job. She endured a dry, lonely, disorienting period of reassembling the somewhat fragmented pieces of her personality. But she eventually emerged with her cardinal qualities of independence, creativity, and curiosity intact and stronger than ever. And her core value of freedom found new ways to express itself.

As she grew stronger, Amy did find ways to support freedom in her community. Her External Fire is currently roaring away, preparing exactly the type of fuel she wants to share with people who need to develop confidence in self-determination and self-expression. Moreover, in her metaphorical home—the places she frequents and the people she sees every day—a beautiful Relational Fire is burning, providing safety, warmth, and comfort.

As you can tell by the way Amy described her current most intimate relationship, that Relational Fire burns with a special fuel, a love that seeks to support her rather than control her. The freedom she values so highly is feeding into the kind of nurturance she craves the most. And I know she feels that the "sun never set on so glorious" a love as the one she now has.

Relational Fire

With Relational Fire, we are drawing the circle of our focus tighter and determining exactly what we find within it. What kind of heat energy will we discover within the circumference we draw around our day-to-day relationships? Will we find a life-giving, comforting, well-tended fire in a fireplace? Or will we find the smoking ruins resulting from carelessly scattered and unchecked sparks?

Within the F.I.R.E.S. personal strategic planning system, External Fire involved defining the contribution you want to make to community at any scale. It was about taking the clarity you developed around your core values and deepest beliefs and doing something about it, starting with the world outside your door.

At this point, you're being asked to step over the threshold of that door and discover what's going on inside. Now is the time to take the temperature of your most significant daily relationships at home, work, or wherever you spend the most time. Relational Fire is all about family, friends, and fellows.

Your family includes your parents, siblings, spouse, significant other, children, close relatives, and maybe even your pets. Regardless of your past or present relationship with each member of your family, these are typically the ones who know you best. They have seen the best—and worst—in you throughout your lifetime. Your family is a source of powerful influence in your life, fueling your development at every level, from personality to worldview.

Your friends and fellows are the people you routinely spend time with. You could see them in casual or recreational environments or in more formal settings, such as the workplace. These "friends and fellows" include everyone from your best friend and closest confidant to your coworkers, colleagues, teammates, and associates. For whatever personal or professional reasons, these relationships hold some level of importance to you, such that you maintain an investment in them.

Family, friends, and fellows are incredible sources of power. If you think of a healthy, healing Relational Fire as that fire in your fireplace that warms your home, you'll get a good idea of what healthy relational dynamics can provide. They fill your life with a feeling of security, comfort, and joy. They exude the energy that makes a house a home.

On the other hand, a raging, untended Relational Fire wreaks havoc where it really hurts. It's a house fire that obliterates your sense of being at home and at peace in the world. Worst of all, it can meaninglessly consume the energy of your core values, depleting you and preventing you from carrying out your desired purposes.

Your External Fire process led you to define the contribution you could make to your community, while your Relational Fire process will help you define the contribution you want to make to family, friends, and fellows. External Fire looks further out and Relational Fire focuses in closer, but they are both tended by an attitude of intention and generosity. In both realms of your life—communal/social and interpersonal/intimate—you need to give to get. External Fire means contributing to community so that you can reap the abundance you want and need. And Relational Fire means contributing to your relationships so you can access the nurturance you want and need.

At the end of this chapter, you will create a strategy to further develop your most important relationships. Like Amy, you want relationships that reflect your core values and allow you to fulfill the purposes that mean the most to you. Like Amy, you want to make the changes necessary to either ameliorate or eliminate relational trends that take away your power to make the contributions you were born to make.

At the end of the chapter, you will continue the personal strategic planning process you started with Spiritual Fire and continued with External Fire. You'll read stories and insights to prime the pumps of your imagination and strategic intelligence. Note that much of the discussion ahead does tend to focus on more intimate relationships, such as marital partnerships, but the principles will still apply to your relationships in general. Intimate relationships provide a more distilled, super-charged version of our relational dynamics in general. I think you'll find the same trends you see in your closest relationships radiate outwards and manifest in your less intimate relationships as well. Like Amy, if you experience a trend of being controlled in your marriage, don't be surprised if you see that dynamic presenting itself in less potent forms in your friendships and work relationships too.

Relationships are complicated. Your closest ones are likely to be the most difficult to analyze or change. Hence, your Relational Fire process is guaranteed to challenge you. This will get you out of your comfort zone. But if you apply yourself to the process with an open mind and heart, you'll create a Relationship Development Strategy that could initiate some truly desirable changes.

At that stage, you will be:

- defining the way you would like to develop your daily relationships with family, friends, and fellows, so that you can create a Relationship Development Strategy

- analyzing your relational situation
- envisioning various scenarios in which you try out various approaches to getting to where you want to go in terms of developing your relationships
- evaluating the solution you chose to figure out whether you're on course towards realizing your Relationship Development Strategy

But before you dig into the reflecting and planning process, let's take a closer look at Relational Fire. Let's start considering how our closest relationships factor into living the lives we're meant to lead.

A Fire Fueled By Kindness, Tended Within Boundaries

If External Fire is about giving abundantly in order to access the abundance you need, Relational Fire is about nurturing intentionally in order to access the nurturance you need. In both, you get what you give.

So as you can see, we're following the same trajectory from Spiritual to External to Relational and onward. First, you defined your core values and deepest beliefs. Then you determined how you wanted to express those values within the community. And now you're going to figure out how to express those values in your closer relationships.

As we discussed in the last chapter, the F.I.R.E.S. system works like this:

1) Focus on your big picture purposes.

2) Express that purpose outwardly in terms of how you care for others.

3) Express that purpose inwardly in terms of how you care for yourself.

We're right in the middle of our journey. We're discovering what it means for that big picture perspective (a focus on values and purposes) to sprinkle throughout all facets of your life.

So what does it mean for your relationships to support your core values by allowing you to thrive? What does it mean for you to be the person you want and need to be within your relationships? What does it mean to nurture your relationships intentionally so that you can draw the nurturance you need from them?

Here's some food for thought.

In 1986, the psychologists John Gottman and Robert Levenson set up "The Love Lab" to study the interactions of newlyweds. They would hook couples up to electrodes that measured their heart rates, blood flow, and sweat production, and ask them questions about their relationship. Then, six years later, they followed up with these couples to find out whether they were still together.

Gottman and Levenson discovered that the couples who were the most physiologically active during their interviews—the ones who sweated more, with faster heart rates—tended to be the ones with the unhappily-ever-after stories. These couples, whom the psychologists dubbed "disasters", either divorced or were unhappy in their marriages.

On the other hand, the couples who maintained calmer physiological states during their Love Lab interviews stayed happily together. These couples were able to talk about the intimate details of their relationship, including conflicts they were facing, without breaking a sweat—literally. Gottman and Levenson nicknamed these couples the "masters".

But what story were those electrodes telling about the couples in the Love Lab? What do pulse rates or a few droplets of sweat have to do with relational success?

Gottman ultimately determined that the physiological data—signs of stress or calm—simply reflected the emotional culture that each of these couples created. The more trusting and intimate the relationship, the more relaxed the couple was in their interactions. But the more strained and distrustful their relational culture, the more stressed they were as they discussed the ins and outs of their lives with the researchers.

In further studies, Gottman continued to examine how masters created their trusting cultures and how disasters created their stressful conditions. He discovered that people in successful relationships tended to cultivate a few simple habits that had profound impacts. Chief among these was a tendency to respond to their spouse's "bids" for connection with interest, respect, and support. For example, if a woman told a story about her day, her husband would listen and ask questions that signaled he was paying attention. Couples who responded positively to one another's bids for connection 87% of the time remained happily together six years after the study. On the other hand, couples who divorced in this same time period tended to respond to their spouse's bids with disinterest, disrespect, or a lack of support 66% of the time.

Kindness, it would seem, is the key. The relationship psychologist Ty Tashiro echoes Gottman's findings in his book *The Science of Happily Ever After*. Therein, he discusses the high correlation between enduringly satisfying relationships and the character trait of "agreeableness": a capacity for warmth, cooperation, sympathy, and tactfulness. Moreover, the significance of kindness extends into all of our successful relationships. Tashiro describes kindness in our friendships as "providing praise after successes, and moral support after failures, and generously giving…with no immediate expectation of payback."

When we look at the science of good relationships, it seems so simple, doesn't it? It appears all the lessons our mothers taught us about "playing nice" were really more astute than we gave them credit for.

But what about those relationships in which—despite your best efforts to be kind, agreeable, supportive, and calmly available—there are still many undesirable elements swirling around? What about those relationships that make our pulses race and cause us to sweat, no matter how kind we are? What if, like my friend Amy, you find yourself in a relationship at work or home that stresses you to the point where you can't express your core values or be the person you want to be?

I'd say, in these situations, kindness is still key. But the kindness in these circumstances looks a little different. Think tough love. Think boundaries.

As Tashiro puts it, all people "have some traits that are less desirable, and those traits can drive us crazy. When those traits go unmitigated and manifest themselves as chronic meanness, cruelty or a lack of concern, then people are right to point out these concerning characteristics and to ask for some mindful changes on the part of the guilty party."

Sometimes the best contribution you can make to a relationship is a courageous setting of boundaries.

Within relationships, a boundary is:

1. A guideline or rule that you create or adopt to show people how they should behave towards you if they want you to feel safe or respected.

2. A sense of how you will respond to people, or what consequences will result, if they ignore those rules or guidelines.

For example, Amy now has a clear boundary regarding lies. The people in her life know (most of them without needing to be told) that she values honesty and transparency. That's their guideline for behaving in a way that will make her feel safe and respected. And Amy knows that if someone in her life consistently ignores that *guideline*, or boundary, she will respond actively, rather than suffer in silence. She will simply exit the relationship. That's the consequence for lying repeatedly to Amy.

Boundaries don't exist—as Amy's former boss probably thought—to keep people separate or to limit intimacy or even sacrificial kindness between them. Rather, they allow people to get and remain close. That's because boundaries support trust. Because Amy knows she has the strength to leave someone who violates her boundaries, she's confident that she can create healthy relationships, rather than settle for less. She's free to approach her current relationships with a willingness to trust. She trusts in herself as well as in the people she is building relationships with.

Furthermore, sometimes kindness-via-boundaries (tough love, if you will) can truly bring out the best in us. Enforcing a boundary doesn't always take the extreme form of leaving a relationship behind. If fact, it usually doesn't. Often, when people exhort us—or actively require us—to do better by them, it can change us for the better.

The psychologist Henry Cloud explained this in his book *Boundaries: When to Say Yes, How to Say No to Take Control of Your Life:* "We change our behavior when the pain of staying the same becomes greater than the pain of changing. Consequences give us the pain that motivates us to change."

The image of a Relational Fire burning in a fireplace to provide warmth, security, and joy to a home becomes more apt the more deeply we investigate successful relationships. Think about it.

The fire needs intentional fuel: sticks of firewood that we cut and set aside specifically for this purpose. Think of this fuel as the kindness Gottman, Tashiro, and many others have described. These sticks of firewood are acts of calm attentiveness, support, and respect. We can feed this fuel to our fire with our every interaction with family, friends, and fellows.

The fire also needs specific boundaries; it burns in a fireplace, rather than rages throughout the whole home. These boundaries are the guidelines we set around how we are to be treated and what consequences will result if these guidelines are ignored. Without them, a fire meant to warm our home becomes a disaster, a force that consumes everything precious to us, including our sense of self.

When you light and tend your Relational Fire—by creating and implementing your Relationship Development Strategy—I want you to consider these two aspects of a home fire. Upon first glance they might seem contradictory, but continuous kindness and consistent boundaries are actual natural counterparts. The kind of nurturance you need in your life will have both aspects. In your best relationships, you'll receive the care and attention you need, but also the clarion call to be your best self. When you make your best contribution to your relationships, it will include facets of both gentle and tough love.

Just remember that the Relational Fire burns in a clearly demarcated fireplace and exudes the warmth of the kindness it feeds on. Build this kind of fire, and you'll always have the nurturance you need.

Your Relational Fire Workbook

Your Relational Fire Process

We have arrived at the Relational Fires stage of your personal strategic planning process. By now, you're an expert at this, right?

You began this process by proactively lighting and tending your Spiritual Fire with a Personal Definition Strategy. You continued that process by lighting and tending your External Fire with a Social Contribution Strategy. Now it's time to draw a smaller circle and focus on the people who are with you on a daily (or near daily) basis. It's time to define how you want your relationships with these family members, friends, and fellows to be—and to start doing what you can to make them so.

Before getting started on the Relational Fire component of your personal strategic planning process, recall that the entire F.I.R.E.S. system looks like this:

F.I.R.E.S.

Financial: You want and need professional/financial security and success

Internal: You want and need a holistically healthy day to day existence

Relational: You want and need good relationships with friends and family

External: You want and need to make social/community contributions

Spiritual: You want and need, above all else, to live out your core values

The entire F.I.R.E.S. process is like taking the biggest picture perspective possible and then gradually narrowing your focus. Hence, you moved from defining your core values and deepest beliefs to determining how to live them out on a larger social scale—and now you're going to figure out how to express those same core values in a more intimate, day-to-day way. In other words, it's time to focus on your "nearest and dearest." The work you will do for the remainder of this chapter will culminate in the creation of a Relationship Development Strategy.

Once again, this section (Your Relational Fire Process) is stylized in workbook form so that you can use its pages to record your thoughts and create your Relationship Development Strategy. If you find the spaces allotted aren't large enough for your notes, please use whatever makes you feel comfortable and stay organized.

Let's do this.

Chapter Four

Your Problem Statement

1. Briefly describe your current relationships with family, friends, and fellows. Are your closest relationships healthy and thriving or damaged and stressful?

2. Briefly describe the relationships you would like to have with family, friends, and fellows. This could include factors such as communication or quality and quantity of time.

3. List any behaviors, patterns, or circumstances in your life that seem to be undermining the types of relationships you want to be developing. What feels contradictory to your values as they relate to your relationships?

4. Summarize your previous answers into a brief sentence or paragraph. Identify any relational challenges or gaps in your life that you wish to overcome. This is your Relational Fire Problem Statement.

Your Vision Statement

1. Think about the best relationship you have with any family member, friend, or fellow. What makes that relationship work so well? What are you both doing to ensure that things continue to go well?

2. Imagine that you are writing an inspirational children's book or a movie script about an ideal family or relationship. Describe the positive interactions, communication, or habits between the main characters that make this group special.

3. Summarize your previous answers into a brief sentence or paragraph. Consider how your vision of the future addresses your Relational Fires Problem Statement. Identify anything that encourages you to strengthen or forge meaningful relationships with your family, friends, and fellows. This is your Relational Fires Vision Statement.

Mission Statement

1. How would you describe the purpose or mission that your Vision Statement seems to be telling you to fulfill within your daily relationships?

2. Briefly list a few actions or endeavors that would concretely fulfill this sense of purpose or mission.

3. Refer back to your Problem Statement and Vision Statement. What specific things must you do now to light and tend your Relational Fire?

4. Summarize your previous answers into a brief, action-oriented sentence or paragraph. This is your Relational Fire Mission Statement.

Your Values and Beliefs

A. Refer back to your Personal Definition Strategy under the Spiritual Fires section. Are there any values that are absent from that list that you now require to accomplish a Social Contribution Strategy? If not, simply transfer those values in the spaces below.

B. Beliefs are your current perspectives, opinions, and conclusions based upon your cumulative knowledge and understanding. Refer back to your Personal Definition Strategy under the Spiritual Fires section. Are there any beliefs that are absent from that list that you now require to accomplish a Social Contribution Strategy? If not, simply transfer those values in spaces below.

Chapter Four

Goals and Objectives

This section of the Relational Fire Process is truly the moment when you can take your third lighter and light a fire that will warm your home.

You now have an opportunity to contemplate which goals you wish to accomplish in the Relational Fires portion of F.I.R.E.S.

In this section, you will be using a model for goal-setting that involves identifying hurdles or challenges, figuring how you will measure your progress, and determining any timelines or deadlines for realizing these goals.

Now, turn the page and define your goals for lighting and tending your Relational Fire.

Set Your Goals

To set your goals, remember that you need to define your barriers, your index (way of measuring success), and your timeframe.

Relational

An example of a Relational goal is:

My goal is to overcome my tendency to argue with my sister (barrier) by giving her five positive comments for every one piece of constructive criticism (index: a metric and a measure), by the end of the year (timeframe).

Briefly write up to 3 goals within the model framework above and then transfer your answers to the next page. On the following page, complete the assignment by writing the 3 necessary steps required (i.e., objectives) to successfully accomplish each goal.

Goal #1

My goal is to: by: by the end of:

Goal #2

My goal is to: by: by the end of:

Goal #3

My goal is to: by: by the end of:

Set Your Objectives

1. My goal is to   by   within

1.1. Objective   1.2. Objective   1.3. Objective

2. My goal is to   by   within

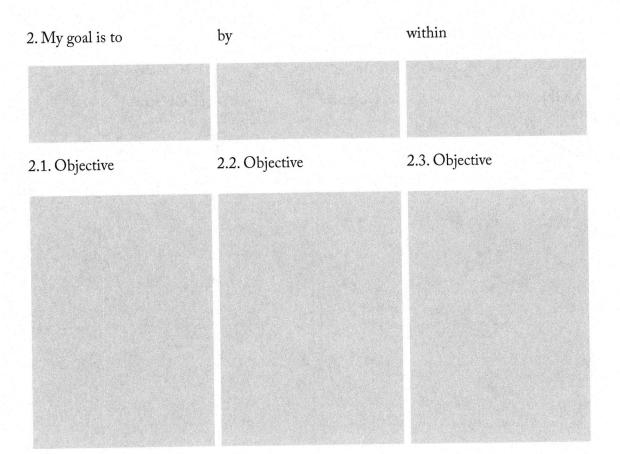

2.1. Objective   2.2. Objective   2.3. Objective

3. My goal is to   by   within

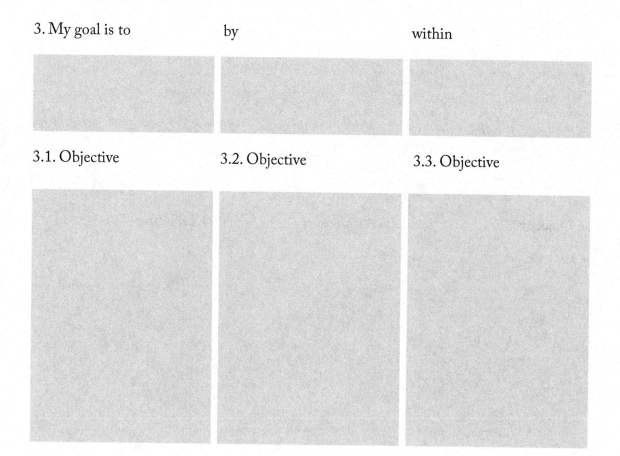

3.1. Objective   3.2. Objective   3.3. Objective

Chapter Four

Your Situational Analysis

1. Transfer your previous Relational Fires Problem Statement here. Feel free to tweak or adjust the statement, if necessary.

2. Consider your Problem Statement. What is your history and present standing with this issue? Write a brief paragraph describing these successes and failures. Provide perspective, background, and insight on where you are coming from.

Your Weaknesses and Strengths

List the 5 main strengths you have that can be used to light and tend your Relational Fire.

1.

2.

3.

4.

5.

List the 5 main weaknesses you have that may present challenges as you light and tend your Relational Fire.

1.

2.

3.

4.

5.

Your Boundaries

When formulating a strategy, there are sometimes boundaries on or limitations to the quality and quantity of alternatives you can feasibly implement.

In the space below, list or describe any resource constraints, prohibitions, concerns or guidelines that might limit your continued formulation of a strategy to light and tend your Relational Fires. This may include time, money, desire, motivation, strengths, weaknesses, opportunities and threats.

Chapter Four

The Scenario Phase

Congratulations on progressing to Phase Three… the Scenario Phase! All of the Relational Fire work you completed up to this point is critically important. Your previous statements and activities will now guide you through brainstorming the possible alternatives and solutions to achieving your desired results.

Problems + Solutions
Goal One

My Relational Fires Problem Statement is:

1 . My goal is to   by   within

1.1. Objective   1.2. Objective   1.3. Objective

Brainstorm possible solutions to your Problem Statement or alternative ways to accomplish your goals here. Circle your best options after you have finished.

Problems + Solutions
Goal Two

My External Fires Problem Statement is:

2. My goal is to   by   within

2.1. Objective   2.2. Objective   2.3. Objective

Brainstorm possible solutions to your Problem Statement or alternative ways to accomplish your goals here. Circle your best options after you have finished.

Problems + Solutions
Goal Three

My External Fires Problem Statement is:

3. My goal is to   by   within

3.1. Objective   3.2. Objective   3.3. Objective

Brainstorm possible solutions to your Problem Statement or alternative ways to accomplish your goals here. Circle your best options after you have finished.

Chapter Four

Think and Reason

Review the possible solutions and alternatives you circled over the last few pages. Why did you choose those circled items and not others to achieve your goals and objectives?

Accountability

How will you remain personally accountable to resolving your Relational Fires Problem Statement and to achieving each goal and objective?

How will you track progress and measure your results? What system of organization or other methodology will you use to collect data and manage improvements?

To ensure a successful completion of your goals and objectives, you will need feedback and focus. Choose an "Accountability Partner" to whom you will regularly communicate progress. This can be a relative, a friend, or another trusted person. We recommend someone (other than your spouse) who will keep your best interests in mind.

Accountability Partner: _____

Accountability Partner: _____

Enough talk...implement!

The following page is a summary sheet of the key statements, goals, and solutions necessary to accomplish your Relationship Development Strategy. Tape a copy of this summary to your bathroom mirror, your refrigerator, or wherever else you need to be reminded of your personal commitment.

Return to this Relational Fires section in a few weeks after your strategy implementation, to re-evaluate your progress and success.

Enough talk... implement!

Relationship Development Strategy

Problem Statement

Vision Statement

Mission Statement

Problem Solutions

Strategy start date: _____

Strategy end date:_____

Accountability Partner:_____

Accountability Partner:_____

1. My goal is to   by   within

1.1. Objective   1.2. Objective   1.3. Objective

2. My goal is to   by   within

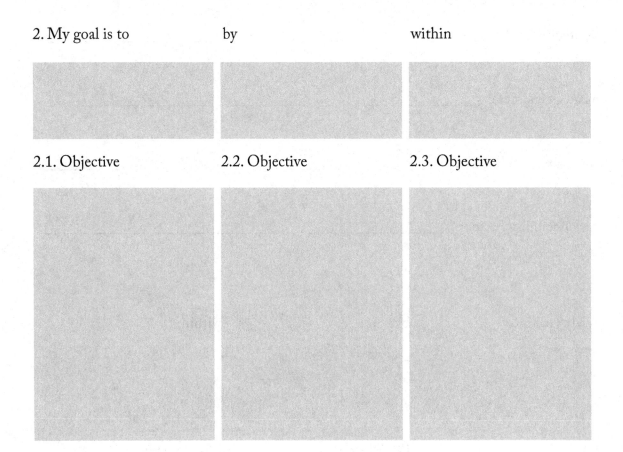

2.1. Objective   2.2. Objective   2.3. Objective

3. My goal is to   by   within

3.1. Objective   3.2. Objective   3.3. Objective

Re-evaluation

1. Now that several weeks have passed since you implemented your Relationship Development Strategy, briefly describe your success in resolving your Relational Fires Problem Statement. Are you celebrating each accomplishment?

2. Refer back to the Relational Fires Vision Statement you wrote describing your desired picture of the future. Is the "future" you are now experiencing anything like you expected back then? Why or why not?

3. What tweaks or changes must you make to your Relationship Development Strategy? Are you on track to resolve your original Relational Fires Problem Statement and related goals? Is it time to repeat these process steps to resolve a new Relational Fires Problem Statement?

Relational Fire: Core Messages

Your Relational Fire is the result of your investment into relationships with family, friends, and fellows.

When you choose to actively light and tend a well-managed Relational Fire, you access the type of nurturance you need in order to be the person you want to be.

Both the fuel of kindness it feeds on and the clearly marked boundaries it burns within define Relational Fire.

Five

Your Internal Fire

Lighting your way, day by day

Fantasies

Often, Susan wouldn't buy much, maybe a few small items. What drew her there—to the mall where she would wander through clothing and furniture stores—was the opportunity to dream.

"I'd think about, 'What if my house looked like this?' or 'What if I looked like that?'" she explains. "When I had free time, that's what I liked to do: go to Nordstrom and de-stress through these fantasies."

And how much "me time" does a working medical doctor and mother of young children have, anyway? That's right: criminally little to nil. What little "Susan time" was available was precious to her. Who could fault her for wanting to spend it in a way that soothed her stress?

What's wrong with a little retail therapy anyway?

But eventually, Susan Gamble, whom I introduced in Chapter 2 as Pastor Matthew's wife, did put her finger on what was wrong with it. One day, she was reading a book an acquaintance from college had written about friendship. A line within it struck her, something about "how so many of us focus on what we look like and not on being likeable and building relationships." It wasn't exactly a revolutionary idea, or one she'd never come across before, but in that moment, it was what she needed to hear.

Susan realized that what she'd been looking for on those fantasy-filled shopping trips was something that she was never going to find in any store. What she needed was connection and acceptance. What she needed was closer relationships with others.

"I realized that by thinking, 'Oh, if I dress a certain way or if my house is furnished a certain way' that, subconsciously, I really was trying to fit in and be accepted by certain groups. And then it hit me: I'm doing it all wrong."

Would Susan even value the people who would "accept" her on such superficial conditions? Were they the kind of folks she would even like or respect? Nobody she'd want to hang out with would like her solely for how she dressed. It was absurd. She was never going to scratch the itch she felt by wandering around a mall.

And it was, Susan realized, a substantial itch, and one she'd felt often over the years. Being a pastor's wife frequently meant exercising a fairly high degree of caution over whom she and Matthew got close to. Despite the fact that, as a couple, they truly valued authenticity—the capability to be "really real"—it was a struggle for them to be fully themselves at times.

That's because, when you're considered a "spiritual leader", people tend to scrutinize your every move. They're on the lookout for "hypocrisy".

When Susan was studying medicine at Yale University, she met a professor who was affiliated with the same religious denomination as she and Matthew were. This was exciting because (as you may remember from Chapter 2) the Gambles didn't often meet folks they could share their spiritual journey with. So Susan pursued a friendship with this professor. That is, until the day she learned this professor had been informing other chief residents about some things that Susan did that "contradicted" her faith.

"We all experience judgment," says Susan. "But if you're in a pastor's family, you're under a magnifying glass."

Feeling gun shy about revealing herself to other people for fear of their judgment brought its own share of loneliness. But living in the Gambles' adopted Californian community brought other challenges as well.

The income drop they experienced when they moved from Florida meant the Gambles weren't exactly in the "upper echelon" of their affluent neighborhood. And when Susan scrolled through her social media feeds, she saw pictures of her friends from residency posing with expensive cars or relaxing in luxurious settings. The "fantasies" on offer throughout her social media channels—unlike the soothing dreams she experienced wandering through malls—sometimes poked her where she was sensitive.

But whether they soothed her, masking her struggles with disconnection, or hurt her, inflaming her sense of isolation, these fantasies weren't doing Susan any favors. She needed to deal with the reality that she felt alone.

Susan decided to set a goal: no shopping for clothes for one year. And that wasn't all. She also started a book club, through which she connected with three "really good girlfriends."

"Now, instead of going shopping, when I have the time, I text these women and we go have lunch, talk, hang out with our kids together," says Susan. "I get a lot of satisfaction out of spending time with other women who are doing what I am doing: pulling off the difficult balancing act of work, family, and self."

This adjustment in how Susan treats her free time—as occasions for reaching out, rather than numbing out—has changed her. She feels a sense of peace that wasn't there before. More than ever, she knows that she is accepted for who she is.

"Nowadays, there is so much opportunity for superficial connection," she says. "It's easy to forget to pursue deeper relationships. But I feel more strongly now that I am growing, and that's because I've chosen to invest in relationships, and let them change me."

The Light Unto Your Feet

There is a bit of poetry in the Psalms about the Scriptures being like "a lamp for my feet, a light for my path." And that's how I like to think about the Internal Fire too. In the metaphor of the five lighters, it's the fourth one, the one that lights the lamp that illuminates your home.

Internal Fire shines a light on the path you walk every day. It gives you a sense of what to do in the small moments that end up meaning everything. Internal Fire gives you an immediate sense of direction in those smaller increments of time—hours or days—when you make choices about how to spend your time and energy. Ultimately, Internal Fire enhances your ability to take the small steps that bring you closer to your ideal for personal development.

With Internal Fire, we are continuing to draw the circle of our focus tighter. With Relational Fire, we started really paying attention to the ins and outs of our daily lives, where the rubber meets the road of our core values. We paid close attention to the qualities and patterns within our most significant relationships. At this point, we're maintaining our gaze on the day-to-day, but we're shifting our attention to one specific place: ourselves.

To adapt the words of Michael Jackson, we're now looking at the (wo)man in the mirror. How do the things you do that are "all about you" contribute to your personal development journey? If you consider the apex of personal development to be living out your core values as fully as possible, how do you make those little daily moments count? How do your health, hobbies, or hopes either support or undermine this journey to becoming the person you want to become?

That's what we'll explore in some detail at this stage of your F.I.R.E.S. experience: how the way you manage your health, the hobbies you develop, and the hopes you pursue take you closer or further away from positive personal development. These "Three H's" of Internal Fire will help you to really zone in on a sense of step-by-step, day-by-day personal development, where the little things become the really big things in the end.

Ultimately, you will create a strategy for self-development that zeroes in on these "little things" that end up being not so little. Like Susan, you'll be taking stock of your "me time" and what it says about who you are becoming. You'll be examining how you tend to spend your self-focused energy: the activities you pursue, the habits you cultivate, and the goals you set that are "just for you".

At the end of the chapter, you will continue the personal strategic planning process you started with Spiritual Fire and continued with External Fire and Relational Fire. We'll take a closer look at this notion of the "Three H's" of Internal Fire. And as always, you'll have the opportunity to read through some stories, research, and insights from experts that should deepen your thinking around these subjects. After that, you'll be ready to take your F.I.R.E.S. journey one step further, with a Personal Development Strategy.

At that stage, you will be:

- defining the way you would like to manage your Three H's, so you can create a Personal Development Strategy

- analyzing your daily personal development situation

- envisioning various scenarios in which you try out various approaches to getting to where you want to go in terms of your daily personal development

- evaluating the solution you chose to figure out whether you're on course towards realizing your Personal Development Strategy

Before you get started on that, are you ready to investigate Internal Fire? Let's take a look at the Three H's and discover what it may reveal to you about your daily progress down the path of personal development.

The Three H's

The whole concept of "personal development" can get pretty amorphous and out there, can't it? However, I believe it largely boils down to the little things that become the big things. I'm a practical man. And I believe how you invest the time and energy that's "just for you" determines so much about the person you are actively becoming. Step by step, you walk by the light of your Internal Fire towards your ultimate self, the person they'll be talking about long after you've passed away. And you can conceive of these daily "steps" in a rather concrete way. Enter the Three H's of Internal Fire.

Health, hobbies, and hopes. These are the three arenas of little things becoming big deals. These are the types of investments that, I believe, really end up constituting the stuff of personal development. So how about a brief rundown of what I mean by each H?

Health— This H is all about what you do to support your mental and physical health. Technically there is a "fourth H" embedded within the "Three H's": holistic, or "concerned with the whole system" that your body and mind constitute. How do you take care of your holistic health?

Hobbies— This H is all about what you do for fun, for a challenge, for learning opportunities, or, in other words, for you. Work, although it can encompass fun, challenges, and learning, and drive major self-development, isn't a hobby. This is about what you do with your "free" time and energy that's strictly focused on you and what matters to you (even when it involves other people).

Hopes—This H is all about the goals you set and the dreams you articulate that are, once again, focused on you. These could be big or small hopes or dreams, short range or long range, simple or complex. They could involve everything from running a marathon to composing a rock opera (more on that later). In achieving these goals and realizing these dreams, you bring yourself closer to becoming the person you dream of becoming.

Are you observing that there can be major overlap among the Three H's? If so, you're entirely right. For example, you might dream of losing fifty pounds. That's a hope. To do that, you need to increase your activity level and consume healthier foods. That's a health issue. So you decide to take a dance class that gets your heart pumping and learn to cook healthy yet delicious meals. Now you're in the hobbies zone.

Yes, the Three H's do tend to overlap. This isn't about rigid compartmentalizing. It's just helpful to think of these H's as starting points for considering how you invest your free, self-focused time and energy. These fairly simple and entirely concrete arenas of attention and time investment are deep drivers of change. Think about how Susan's retail therapy hobby was actually taking her further away from becoming the person she wanted to become. Consider how a simple adjustment in how she spent her "me time" allowed her to start realizing a major goal of hers: developing deeper friendships.

The little things become big deals. So let's take a closer look at these "little things".

Health

For many of us, taking care of our physical and mental health is the priority that never really seems to be addressed. That's because the way we manage our holistic health tends to be solidly grounded in habits—many of which are not so great for us. If our health goals are clear—eat breakfast, get 8 hours of sleep, meditate, workout 4-5 times a week—the way to achieving them often is not.

Consider Susan once again. Her retail therapy habit ended up being a mental health issue. Once she wrapped her head around what she was seeking out of those shopping excursions and what they actually delivered, she could see that plainly. Addressing this health issue became a simple-to-understand and somewhat-challenging-to-execute matter of establishing a new habit: allocating free time towards reaching out to friends rather than to visiting stores.

It turns out that the process Susan underwent to start managing her holistic health the way she wanted to aligns perfectly with what science tells us about habits. As the New York Times business reporter Charles Duhigg describes it in his book *The Power of Habit*, breaking a habit and forming a new habit in its place boils down to cues, rewards, and routines.

First, you experience a cue, a situation or experience that arouses your inclination to engage in a habit. It could be something as obvious as an upsetting emotion or as innocuous as the recurrence of a certain time of day. Next, you identify which reward your habit delivers to you, and try to find a different habit that seems to provide the same reward. Finally, you simply start responding to the old cue with the new habit to receive the old reward, thereby establishing a new routine.

Formerly, when Susan had free time (cue) she would go shopping (old habit). But once she realized she was trying to attain a sense of connection (reward) through shopping, she decided to replace shopping with reaching out to friends (routine). It's simple and it works; but determining what reward you are trying to get through your "bad habits" is key.

Just ask yourself, "Bottom line: what pay-off am I seeking and can I experiment with healthy ways to achieve that?" I think you'll find that you will make better plans to manage all aspects of your health when armed with this question. And once new routines are established, you'll have a lot less thinking to do. (What a relief!)

Hobbies

The word amateur gets short shrift in my opinion. Derived from the French word for "lover", it literally means doing something for love rather than for money. How much of your life is about love rather than money? But if love—or fun, play, intrigue, or adventure—doesn't do it for you, it turns out hobbies can actually make you happier and more productive.

San Francisco State's Dr. Kevin Eschleman has studied the effect of creative hobbies on over 400 employees. He discovered that workers who spend part of their downtime doing something creative, such as sewing or cooking, perform better at work and feel better at home. They are more likely to be collaborative and creative in their job performance and to generally feel a sense of relaxation and control over their lives.

It turns out that taking time to express and discover yourself is never a waste of energy. On the contrary, it generates energy.

For me, the hobby that drives that sense of peaceful personal mastery is music. It's true: this left-brained strategy nerd is also a band geek. I learned to play the trumpet in fourth grade and continued on with band, marching band, and even jazz band throughout high school. In my sophomore year of college, I taught myself how to play acoustic guitar and wrote my first song.

That process—expressing myself, playing around with chords, finding my way through the creation of a song nobody has ever sung before—was thrilling. Then and now, writing and playing music helps me to refocus and to release creative energy. Whether I'm practicing a new guitar riff or expressing myself through the written word, I find music to be limitless and without borders. It represents an evolution of ideas, thoughts, and expressions with no fixed endpoint. In this way, my musical journey runs parallel to my personal development.

As much as I loved (and still love) writing songs, I discovered sharing and performing them with others was even better. After playing on my own for a number of years, several friends and I formed a short-lived band. We even made a few recordings. That experience definitely put the bug in me to eventually produce a more substantial recording project. In fact, over the years, I wrote the music and lyrics for an entire album that has not yet been recorded. My goal is to someday collect the right group of musicians to perform and record the songs.

And that brings us nicely to hopes…

Chapter Five

Hopes

Where do our hopes and dreams come from? What do they say about us? As famed personal trainer Greg Anderson says, "When we are motivated by goals that have deep meaning, by dreams that need completion, by pure love that needs expressing, then we truly live."

I believe truly healthy people have dreams that have nothing to do with making money or fulfilling what others want for them. Part of "truly living" means generating and exploring hopes and dreams that come equipped with repositories of rich and deep personal meaning. And I believe that there are powerful linkages between these individuals' core values and the hopes and dreams they hold that are "just for them".

If you always dreamed of climbing a mountain, why is that? Is it because the cardiovascular gains would be considerable? Is it because that feat would make for great social media fodder? Or might it have something to do with the person you dream of becoming? Who is this person who climbs mountains? Is this mountain-climber determined, powerful, and courageous? Do those qualities in any way reflect your core values or your vision for personal development?

Personal hopes aren't the fluffy "extras" of life. Dreams aren't the things that are nice if you have the time for them. They really matter if you want to truly live. And they will show you, more clearly than most things, what you actually value and who you truly want to become.

I know that ultra-busy lifestyles and a million competing demands have the effect of squeezing out dreams that are "just for you". But it's worth making space for them. What could you do to rouse, revive, or reconstitute the dreams and hopes that reflect your yearning for personal development?

Perhaps try looking way back—and then way ahead.

To start, think back to your childhood and try to remember who you dreamed of becoming "when you grew up." What sort of person did you like to dress up as or pretend to be? Are there any threads connecting that childish desired identity with the core values you currently hold? Examine those linkages to look for enduring themes in your life: aspects of your personality you long to develop, curiosities you long to satisfy, or gifts you long to give to the world or to yourself.

Then, when you have some sense of those enduring themes that extend all the way to the beginning, imagine the end. Habit 2 from Steven Covey's *7 Habits of Highly Effective People* is: Begin with the end in mind. As Covey puts it: "Habit 2 is based on imagination—the ability to envision in your mind what you cannot at present see with your eyes."

If you have a personal goal, a long held hope, or a recurring dream, try to deeply, earnestly, and carefully imagine its fulfillment. What does fulfilling this goal, hope, or dream bring into your life? How does it change you? Does it bring you closer to living in alignment with your core values? Begin with the end in mind and you just might be motivated enough to bring it about.

In my case, I believe that recording my album does align with what I value the most, as well as with the person I envision myself becoming. As someone who is committed to transparency, the act of sharing myself through song feels deeply rewarding. As someone who values his spiritual life, music is an incredibly effective tool for meditation, reflection, and worship. My musical hobbies and hopes—and the holistic health benefits they provide—are fuel in that "lamp unto my feet". It may not make me any money, but music leads me, step by step, on that daily path towards personal development.

Dream on—and then get planning.

Your Internal Fire Workbook

Your Internal Fire Process

It's time to tackle your Internal Fire process. We're drawing the circle tighter and tighter, and it might be challenging to take a hard look at yourself. Fortunately, by now you're an old hand at the process of personal strategic planning.

This all started with your Spiritual Fire process and its Personal Definition Strategy. You continued that process by lighting and tending your External Fire with a Social Contribution Strategy and your Relational Fire with a Relationship Development Strategy. Now it's time to focus on you and the person you're choosing to become with your self-focused time and energy. It's time to define how you want your health, hobbies, and hopes to bring you closer to becoming the person you want to become.

Before getting started on the Internal Fire component of your personal strategic planning process, recall that the entire F.I.R.E.S. system looks like this:

F.I.R.E.S.

Financial: You want and need professional/financial security and success

Internal: You want and need a holistically healthy day to day existence

Relational: You want and need good relationships with friends and family

External: You want and need to make social/community contributions

Spiritual: You want and need, above all else, to live out your core values

The entire F.I.R.E.S. process is like taking the biggest picture perspective possible and then gradually narrowing your focus. Hence, you moved from defining your core values and deepest beliefs to determining how to live them out on a larger social scale. Then, you figured out how to express those same core values in a more intimate, day-to-day way. And now, it's time to ensure that your personal development efforts—which really come into play through though Internal Fire's "Three Hs"—are in alignment with everything else you're building. To that end, the work you will do for the remainder of this chapter will culminate in the creation of a Personal Development Strategy.

To reach that point, remember that you will be working through this strategy formulation model:

Once again, this section (Your Internal Fire Process) is stylized in workbook form so that you can use its pages to record your thoughts and create your Personal Development Strategy. But as always, feel free to use whatever document makes you feel comfortable and helps you stay organized.

Let's get started.

Your Problem Statement

1. When you were a child, you had certain dreams and hopes for your future. Perhaps this included a certain body type, a particular profession, world travel, or some level of education. As a child, what did you hope for or want more than anything?

2. Consider your holistic health, your hobbies, and your hopes or dreams for the future. Mark your present level of satisfaction for each:

Income		Expense		Job	
Most satisfied	☐	Most satisfied	☐	Most satisfied	☐
Satisfied	☐	Satisfied	☐	Satisfied	☐
Least satisfied	☐	Least satisfied	☐	Least satisfied	☐

3. List any behaviors, patterns, or circumstances in your life that seem to be undermining your personal development. What feels contradictory to your values as they relate to the health practices, hobbies, and hopes that lead you, step by step, towards becoming the person you want to be?

4. Summarize your previous answers into a brief sentence or paragraph. Identify any barriers or obstacles to your personal development that you wish to overcome. This is your Internal Fire Problem Statement.

Your Vision Statement

1. It is now 5 years in the future. What have you accomplished in terms of your Internal Fires? What amazing transformation occurred in you these last 5 years?

2. You are now flipping through the photo album of your successful life, as an accomplished old man or woman. You have nothing left to prove to yourself or to the world. In terms of your health, hobbies, and hopes, describe that one photo that still makes you smile after all these years.

3. Summarize your previous answers into a brief sentence or paragraph. Consider how your vision of the future addresses your Internal Fires Problem Statement. Identify anything that encourages you to leap out of bed each morning. This is your Internal Fires Vision Statement.

Your Mission Statement

1. Consider your overall physical, mental, and emotional health. What obvious or subtle changes are necessary in your daily life as it impacts your personal development and overall health? Describe anything that conflicts with your core values.

2. Briefly list a few actions or endeavors that would initiate these necessary changes.

3. Refer back to your Problem Statement and Vision Statement. What specific things must you do now to light and tend your Internal Fire?

4. Summarize your previous answers into a brief, action-oriented sentence or paragraph. This is your Internal Fire Mission Statement.

Your Values and Beliefs

A. Refer back to your Personal Definition Strategy under the Spiritual Fires section. Are there any values that are absent from that list that you now require to accomplish a Personal Development Strategy? If not, simply transfer those values in the spaces below.

B. Beliefs are your current perspectives, opinions, and conclusions based upon your cumulative knowledge and understanding. Refer back to your Personal Definition Strategy under the Spiritual Fires section. Are there any beliefs that are absent from that list that you now require to accomplish a Personal Development Strategy? If not, simply transfer those values in spaces below.

Goals and Objectives

This section of the Internal Fire Process is truly the moment when you can take your fourth lighter and light a fire that will illuminate the way forward.

You now have an opportunity to contemplate which goals you wish to accomplish in the Internal Fires portion of F.I.R.E.S.

In this section, you will be using a model for goal-setting that involves identifying hurdles or challenges, figuring how you will measure your progress, and determining any timelines or deadlines for realizing these goals.

Now, turn the page and define your goals for lighting and tending and tending your Internal Fire.

Set Your Goals

To set your goals, remember that you need to define your barriers, your index (way of measuring success), and your timeframe.

Internal

An example of an Internal goal is:

My goal is to overcome my high blood pressure (barrier) by working out 4-5 times a week (index: a metric and a measure), by the end of the month (timeframe).

Briefly write up to 3 goals within the model framework above and then transfer your answers to the next page. On the following page, complete the assignment by writing the 3 necessary steps required (i.e., objectives) to successfully accomplish each goal.

Goal #1

My goal is to: by: by the end of:

Goal #2

My goal is to: by: by the end of:

Goal #3

My goal is to: by: by the end of:

Set Your Objectives

1. My goal is to   by   within

1.1. Objective   1.2. Objective   1.3. Objective

2. My goal is to   by   within

2.1. Objective   2.2. Objective   2.3. Objective

3. My goal is to   by   within

3.1. Objective   3.2. Objective   3.3. Objective

Your Situational Analysis

1. Transfer your previous Internal Fires Problem Statement here. Feel free to tweak or adjust the statement, if necessary.

2. Consider your Problem Statement. What is your history and present standing with this issue? Write a brief paragraph describing these successes and failures. Provide perspective, background, and insight on where you are coming from.

Your Weaknesses and Strengths

List the 5 main strengths you have that can be used to light and tend your Internal Fire.1.

1.

2.

3.

4.

5.

F.I.R.E.S.

List the 5 main weaknesses you have that may present challenges as you light and tend your Internal Fire.

1.

2.

3.

4.

5.

Chapter Five

Your Boundaries

When formulating a strategy, there are sometimes boundaries on or limitations to the quality and quantity of alternatives you can feasibly implement.

In the space below, list or describe any resource constraints, prohibitions, concerns or guidelines that might limit your continued formulation of a strategy to light and tend your Internal Fires. This may include time, money, desire, motivation, strengths, weaknesses, opportunities and threats.

The Scenario Phase

Congratulations on progressing to Phase Three… the Scenario Phase! All of the Internal Fire work you completed up to this point is critically important. Your previous statements and activities will now guide you through brainstorming the possible alternatives and solutions to achieving your desired results.

Problems + Solutions
Goal One

My Internal Fires Problem Statement is:

1 . My goal is to   by   within

1.1. Objective   1.2. Objective   1.3. Objective

Brainstorm possible solutions to your Problem Statement or alternative ways to accomplish your goals here. Circle your best options after you have finished.

Problems + Solutions
Goal Two

My External Fires Problem Statement is:

2. My goal is to   by   within

2.1. Objective   2.2. Objective   2.3. Objective

Brainstorm possible solutions to your Problem Statement or alternative ways to accomplish your goals here. Circle your best options after you have finished.

Problems + Solutions
Goal Three

My External Fires Problem Statement is:

3. My goal is to   by   within

3.1. Objective   3.2. Objective   3.3. Objective

Brainstorm possible solutions to your Problem Statement or alternative ways to accomplish your goals here. Circle your best options after you have finished.

Think and Reason

Review the possible solutions and alternatives you circled over the last few pages. Why did you choose those circled items and not others to achieve your goals and objectives?

Chapter Five

Accountability

How will you remain personally accountable to resolving your External Fires Problem Statement and to achieving each goal and objective?

How will you track progress and measure your results? What system of organization or other methodology will you use to collect data and manage improvements?

To ensure a successful completion of your goals and objectives, you will need feedback and focus. Choose an "Accountability Partner" to whom you will regularly communicate progress. This can be a relative, a friend, or another trusted person. We recommend someone (other than your spouse) who will keep your best interests in mind.

Accountability Partner: _____

Accountability Partner: _____

Enough talk…implement!

The following page is a summary sheet of the key statements, goals, and solutions necessary to accomplish your Personal Development Strategy. Tape a copy of this summary to your bathroom mirror, your refrigerator, or wherever else you need to be reminded of your personal commitment.

Return to this Internal Fires section in a few weeks after your strategy implementation, to re-evaluate your progress and success.

Enough talk… implement!

Personal Development Strategy

Problem Statement

Vision Statement

Mission Statement

Problem Solutions

F.I.R.E.S.

Strategy start date: _____

Strategy end date: _____

Accountability Partner: _____

Accountability Partner: _____

1. My goal is to   by   within

1.1. Objective   1.2. Objective   1.3. Objective

2. My goal is to   by   within

2.1. Objective   2.2. Objective   2.3. Objective

3. My goal is to   by   within

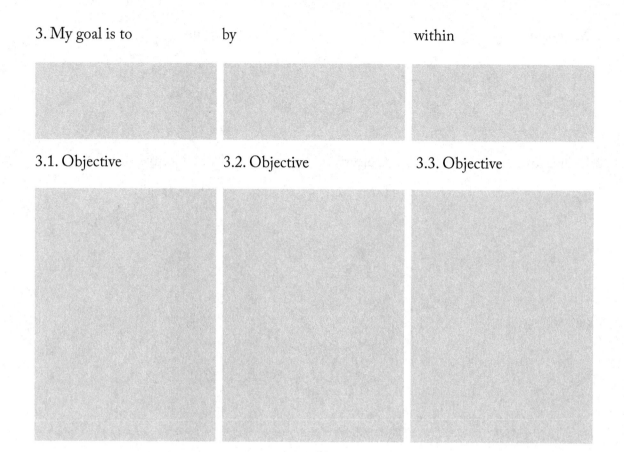

3.1. Objective   3.2. Objective   3.3. Objective

Chapter Five

Re-evaluation

1. Now that several weeks have passed since you implemented your Personal Development Strategy, briefly describe your success in resolving your Internal Fires Problem Statement. Are you celebrating each accomplishment?

2. Refer back to the Internal Fires Vision Statement you wrote describing your desired picture of the future. Is the "future" you are now experiencing anything like you expected back then? Why or why not?

3. What tweaks or changes must you make to your Personal Development Strategy? Are you on track to resolve your original Internal Fires Problem Statement and related goals? Is it time to repeat these process steps to resolve a new Internal Fires Problem Statement?

Internal Fire: Core Messages

Your Internal Fire is the result of where you invest your self-focused, free time and energy; it's about what you do for you.

When you choose to actively light and tend a well-managed Internal Fire, you ensure that the things you do for you are bringing you closer to becoming the person you want to become.

The "stuff" of your Internal Fire is found in the way you manage your holistic health, the hobbies you pursue, and the hopes you hold regarding personal goals and dreams.

Six

Your Financial Fire

Stoking the flames of security

The Best Bet

When you think about the moments when you realized the extent of your personal power, how often do rollerblades factor in?

When I was a young man, everything was about extreme sports. I had a pack of friends who all felt the same way. In between dating, hanging out, and forming the identities that would carry us through adulthood, we paint-balled, rock climbed, and rollerbladed like maniacs.

Harold, our church's youth group leader, was a man of adventure himself, a world traveler and a seasoned entrepreneur. And he knew a good lesson when he saw one. So one day he said, "While you're out there leaving your skin on sidewalks, why don't you take the opportunity to do something big?"

What could that be? We pondered it a while and then landed on a plan. We'd rollerblade all over Philadelphia looking for coins to give to Harold to do "something big". We went everywhere—we had no shame! We stuck our fingers into public telephone slots, video game coin returns, and under drive-through windows after hours. After a few months, our collective efforts generated hundreds of dollars in coins—all packed into empty Cool Whip tubs that we brought to Harold.

He said, "Now let me show you what money can do." He was never specific about the details, but we found out later that on one of his adventures in Africa, he put a roof on a church with the money.

It was the first time I experienced something powerful being generated out of something small and throwaway. A bunch of kids on rollerblades, a few buckets of lost coins, and people's lives half a world away could be impacted in a significant way. We just needed someone like Harold to inspire us to think about our time and energy differently.

Fast forward to the days when I decided to leave my tech industry job to buy the juice bar. I had been earning Fortune 500 money, but I just had to go out on my own. I made contact with the local juice bar I frequented, and the owners and I decided to go into business together. I took the money I had, negotiated deals, and made it happen.

I was scared. But I stepped out in faith. Something was leading me out of my familiar routines and into the realm of calculated risk.

Ultimately the juice bar business tripled in sales after the first year. When I sold the business half a decade later, I more than recouped my investment—and I had vastly exceeded my previous Fortune 500 salary.

After that, when I returned to a different corporate job for the benefits I wanted as a young father, I did feel a level of security I'd been missing. I didn't have to work quite so hard. There was consistency. But I missed creating my own structures and rules. So I found ways to keep following my entrepreneurial bent.

Currently, I run three businesses. In April 2017, I left my last "steady job" to focus on these interests. My newest venture is a human resources company that puts people to work. As I write this Chapter, we've been open for five weeks and I haven't made a dime. But everything is headed in the right direction. I see the reward ahead of me. I have enough corporate and entrepreneurial experience to know that I can do anything I put my mind to, as long as it's the right thing.

This work is the right thing for my family and me. I've already done well enough financially to feel secure. And I'm not looking to become wealthy; I just want to put three kids through braces and college. The bottom line is that today, among other things, I am reducing the barriers between people and work. That's priceless to me.

With the decisions I've made, I support my family, I live out my core values, and I create the conditions for the best life I could lead. It's scary to take risks, but if you think about it, certain risks are no-brainers.

If I took the Steady Eddie approach and clung to employment, going through the layoffs and the relocations, the risks wouldn't be worth the rewards. But carefully and systematically building lifestyle businesses—even if they necessitate serious up-front investments of finances and energy—is more than worth it.

I would rather have hundreds of paychecks rather than just one. Depend on one employer? No, thank you. Depend on hundreds of clients? That's more like it.

And ultimately, the best bet I could make is on myself.

Harold knew it back then: even a bunch of ruffians on rollerblades can do something big if they adjust their thinking and behavior ever so slightly. What can a grown man with a lot of experience, insight, willingness to work, and clarity around his values do?

It's not rocket science. It's belief.

A Ring of Security

Let's take a moment to look back, and take it all in.

Once upon a time, you were living in a place where the unruly fires of spiritual confusion, social disengagement, relational stress, personal neglect, and financial/professional chaos came together to create a massive conflagration. Your home and everything around it was being consumed. You ran around ineffectually beating at the flames. Your life was devoted to fighting fires you could never completely extinguish.

But then the fire died down and you were given a second chance. You walked up to five lighters suspended in mid air, and intentionally used each one to light functional fires around your property.

You used the first lighter to start a controlled burn of the clutter and tangled vegetation that had accumulated around your property. This cleared away the confusion that once obscured your Spiritual vision. You uncovered a deep clarity around your deepest beliefs and core values.

You used the second lighter to start a fire in a large brick oven in the courtyard. This allowed you to prepare a meal for community at any scale you chose. You had a sense of what you wanted your social contribution to be.

You used the third lighter to start a fire in the fireplace that warms your home. This allowed you to focus on creating warm, life-giving relationships of reciprocal nurturing. You knew how you wanted to develop your relationships with friends, family, and fellows.

You used the fourth lighter to light a lantern that illuminates your home. This "lamp unto your feet" helped you to make better decisions in your daily life as it concerned your health, hobbies, and hopes. You understood how the little things become the big things when it comes to your personal development.

Now, you are about to use the fifth lighter to light the torches that surround your property and keep predatory animals away. You are about to light and tend your Financial Fire. And why do you do this?

You do it to secure everything we have just taken stock of. The grounds, the home, the capability to serve the community, your very self…it all must be protected if it is to be enjoyed. Financial Fire is a fire of security that surrounds and supports everything else you have invested into, making all the good things in your life possible—and ultimately, sustainable.

How do you define professional and financial success? Is it about power, growth, and pure metrics? Do you know you're headed in the right direction simply because you can count the number of rungs you've climbed?

Or does professional and financial success only become meaningful in the context of a life well lived? In other words, do your work and the way you manage your money cohere with the other values-driven aspects of your life? Is your work and money there to express, reflect, or protect your ability to live out your core values? Do your profession and finances serve your life—or do they use the rest of your life as mere fuel so they can burn out of control?

You don't want to light and tend the other four fires of personal mastery just to see everything go up in flames again. Rather, you want to create a ring of security around the incredibly valuable aspects of your life that you are investing into.

Financial Fire is that ring of protective torches. It guides you in developing your career and managing your finances so that you can support, sustain, and secure your balanced, values-driven life. Financial Fire gives you clarity around your professional goals, so that your personal development doesn't go on pause at the office. It also helps you develop your financial management skills so you can take care of yourself and others, and continue your personal development journey the way you want to.

At this juncture of the F.I.R.E.S. journey, you must ask yourself, "Does it all fit together? Do my Spiritual, External, Relational, and Internal strategies find a stable foundation in my work and finances? Will the center hold?" You will see how well your work and money management cohere with the other value-driven aspects of your life. And you will get the opportunity to determine just how deeply you resonate—or could resonate—with these words from the English philosopher Lawrence Pearsall Jacks:

A master in the art of living draws no sharp distinction between his work and his play; his labor and his leisure; his mind and his body; his education and his recreation. He hardly knows which is which. He simply pursues his vision of excellence through whatever he is doing, and leaves others to determine whether he is working or playing. To himself, he always appears to be doing both.

At the end of the chapter, you will continue the personal strategic planning process you started with Spiritual Fire and continued with External Fire, Relational Fire, and Internal Fire. Once again, you'll explore thinking and research around the topics of professional and financial success so that you can enter into the planning process inspired and fired up. Finally, you'll conclude your F.I.R.E.S. journey with a Professional Development Strategy.

At that stage, you will be:

- defining the professional goals you want to set and financial management practices you want to adopt, so you can create a Professional Development Strategy

- analyzing your financial/professional situation

- envisioning various scenarios in which you try out various approaches to getting to where you want to go in terms of your profession and finances

- evaluating the solution you chose to figure out whether you're on course towards realizing your Professional Development Strategy

First, let's investigate Financial Fire. It's time to consider the place work and finances have in our lives—and whether it's time for a change.

Necessary Evils and Unsolvable Problems

When I say "work" and "finances", what do you feel? A swell of satisfaction? A tickle of pride? A rush of peace?

If you're an American, the chances are fairly good that you don't feel any of these things. In fact, you're just as likely to feel a thud of ennui, a frisson of anxiety, and a weight of depression.

According to the Conference Board Business Association's latest (2016) employment satisfaction survey, a little less than 50% of Americans are satisfied with their current jobs. (Sadly, that's actually an 11-year high for American job satisfaction!) People all over the country are spending the lion's share of their time in environments and roles that don't suit them, don't help them grow, and don't make them wake up in the morning excited.

But even if these people detest their jobs, making a change is hard when the wolves are pawing at the door. For all too many Americans, debt is a stark reality. A 2016 Nerdwallet study found the average American household is $135,924 in debt. The average household with credit card debt owes $16,425, and is on the hook for $1,300 a year in interest. And that's not just bad for the economy—it's bad for the soul.

In fact, several clinical studies have established a link between debt and major mental illnesses. The University of South Hampton published a report in Clinical Psychology Review that reviewed 65 studies on debt and mental health. Among their findings, they discovered indebted people are three times more likely to have mental health problems like anxiety, depression, psychotic disorders, and substance abuse issues. Moreover, victims of "successful" suicides are eight times more likely to have been in debt.

When you mix low job satisfaction with stressful financial conditions, what do you get? How about the feeling that work is a necessary evil, and money is an unsolvable problem? Am I describing the conditions for a raging inferno that consumes rather than conserves, a Financial Fire that could turn any one of us into a haggard firefighter?

For many of us, the professional and financial arenas of our lives epitomize the "wildfire" mode of living. The power and potential of work and money creates destructive blazes we have to spend all of our time and energy fighting. Perhaps, out of all the Fires, it is most difficult to harness the Financial Fire rather than suffer its unmanaged and out of control effects. It's a serious challenge to reframe Financial Fire as a force that can protect and sustain us, when we've spent years trying to stamp out its deleterious effects.

How are you supposed to feel sustained and protected by a job you dislike and a financial situation that erodes your well-being? How could you ever become the "Master of Living" Lawrence Pearsall Jacks envisioned: the person who "draws no sharp distinction between his work and his play"? That seems like a tall order, doesn't it?

Perhaps, as with most things, it begins in the mind.

Mindsets of the Masters of Living

Self-made millionaire Robert Kiyosaki famously said that "the rich don't work for money", but money does work for the rich. In his best-selling book *Rich Dad, Poor Dad*, he outlines all the ways in which the rich and the poor experience different financial outcomes because of their markedly different mindsets.

In Kiyosaki's experience, the rich engage in a number of wealth-making behaviors that the poor do not. And these behaviors reflect a particular perspective on money and work. For example, the poor will spend their energy working hard at a job to "get by". But the rich will spend their energy becoming more financially literate and making investments that create ongoing passive income. Among the poor, sensitivity to scarcity fuels the dogged application of nose to grindstone. Among the rich, sensitivity to reward fuels a habit of taking calculated risks.

Are you that indebted "poor dad" who clings to a particular job because it alleviates the fear that your difficult conditions have instilled in you? Is it possible you come from a family or a community of people who have learned to associate work and money with stress? Is debt-related mental health distress a theme in your life or that of your family or close friends? Do you have a lot of emotion tied up in your work and finances that might be crowding out your ability to reason and think—and actually improve your situation?

According to Kiyosaki and many other financial success thinkers, making that mindset switch from fear to logic can make all the difference in the world. The fact is your professional and financial situation can very likely be optimized for better outcomes. You just have to turn down the dial on your fear and start believing in your own ability to reason. Take me as an example: I need to take risks to create my ideal situation, but these risks are based on careful planning and sound analysis. Only fear would prevent me from seizing the opportunities that my logic has revealed to me.

Once you start navigating with reason rather than fear, where could you go professionally and financially? Could you bring yourself a little closer to operating like that Master in the Art of Living? Why not start by asking yourself a simple question: What do I want to do and how much will it cost to do it?

For example, the efficiency expert Tim Ferriss talks about "ideal lifestyle costing". He argues that for most people, their ideal lifestyle— one full of experiences, opportunities to learn, and positive self-development—is closer than they think. He recommends a simple exercise: list monthly expenses, create "dreamlines" with the characteristics and costs of an "ideal life", and determine the "Target Monthly Income" that will support all of it.

I've done something similar and it's given me the confidence to step out as an entrepreneur when I've needed to. Three sets of braces and three college tuitions. I don't exaggerate my costs and in turn, I don't exaggerate my fears or my need for "stable employment".

Ferriss argues that most people think in terms of annual income, becoming attached to the idea of occupying the income brackets that they associate with their ideal lifestyles. But in most cases, the life that people would truly enjoy costs less than they think. The Target Monthly Income exercise can make that clear. After all, within those enviable and impressive income brackets, people are frequently living truly wasteful lives. They spend more energy on projects that don't yield good results. They spend more money on possessions that don't truly excite them or inspire growth. They measure their professional and financial "success" by two highly suspect metrics: how many hours they log at work and the number of zeros in their annual salary.

Think back to our discussion of Internal Fire and the sacred role of the criminally underrated "hobby". Hobbies can make us more productive and happy, enhancing efficiency. When we're more productive and happy, we are much less likely to fall into what the sociologist Juliet Schor calls the "work-spend-work-spend mentality". That is to say, working "harder"—i.e., spending more time at work—generates more money to buy the stuff that ends up feeding our depression. This then makes us work even harder to earn even more money to buy even more of the stuff that we believe will salve our stressed-out souls. It's a vicious cycle.

One means of escaping this cycle is to do what Ferris espouses and create a logical plan for an "ideal lifestyle" that includes the experiences that enrich our souls. And then shaving off the unnecessary stuff: the waste, the over-consumption, and the emotional and financial efficiency leaks that result from the "work-spend-work-spend mentality". Recall, if you will, Susan's story. That's just one example of a person who fixed an efficiency leak that resulted from trying to address an emotional need with material products.

Fortunately, having taken your F.I.R.E.S. journey all the way from Spiritual to Internal Fire, you have a lot of clarity over what your "ideal lifestyle" could look like. You have a strong sense of how you want your core values to guide your life. You know what that values-driven life looks like in terms of your community involvement, your daily relationships, and your self-focused time. Now you just need to figure out how to fund that. Now you just need to create a ring of protective torches burning with Financial Fire around that lifestyle. You need to keep the "wolves" away from the balanced, healthy, and values-oriented life that is leading you towards becoming the person you want to become.

I hope by now you see that these wolves are not just manifest in the hard realities of debt, financial stresses, and professional dissatisfactions. Those types of wolves are there, and they truly do have sharp teeth. They will snatch your time, energy, and spiritual focus away from you if they are able. But the wolves you really need to ward off are the ones that emerge from your mind. These are the wolves who whisper that "more" is always the answer: more hard work, more time at the office, more money, and more possessions.

When you light a protective Financial Fire, you call upon the wise, grounded, clear-sighted, and values-driven part of you that can see through this lie. You are able to make logical plans for supporting your lifestyle. You are able to eliminate wasteful efficiency leaks that take you off your spiritual track.

Kiyosaki and Ferriss recommend exploiting opportunities to generate passive income as a way to free up time and secure funds. And both see mindset as a major obstacle to perceiving and capitalizing on those opportunities. According to Ferriss, "people will choose unhappiness over uncertainty." They will prefer the familiar agony of the grindstone to the undiscovered country of taking intelligent risks and making necessary changes.

Perhaps you've already started pondering what those intelligent risks and necessary changes should be as it concerns your work and how you manage money. Maybe you perked up when I mentioned Ferriss' and Kiyosaki's endorsement of passive income and you want to know more. Now, the scope of this book won't allow me to cover a subject like passive income—but keep that fire in your belly to learn more burning. It's the first spark of the Financial Fire that burns to protect and support your ideal life, rather than consume your time, energy, and well-being. It's the first spark of a commitment to problem-solving, rather than mindless grindstone fixation.

And now it's time to feed that spark.

Your Financial Fire Workbook

Your Financial Fire Process

Are you ready for the last component of your personal strategic planning process? We have arrived at Financial Fire. It's the moment you'll take a hard look at your professional and financial situation, and create a strategy for moving forward in these areas. By now, you know exactly how to do that.

This all started with your Spiritual Fire process and its Personal Definition Strategy. You continued that process by lighting and tending your External Fire with a Social Contribution Strategy, your Relational Fire with a Relationship Development Strategy, and your Internal Fire with a Personal Development Strategy. You're now ready to gain clarity around your professional goals, and develop your financial management skills. This will allow you to take care of yourself and others, and to continue your personal development journey the way you want to.

Before getting started on the Financial Fire component of your personal strategic planning process, recall that the entire F.I.R.E.S. system looks like this:

F.I.R.E.S.

Financial:	You want and need professional/financial security and success
Internal:	You want and need a holistically healthy day to day existence
Relational:	You want and need good relationships with friends and family
External:	You want and need to make social/community contributions
Spiritual:	You want and need, above all else, to live out your core values

We started with a big picture perspective: defining the core values that must guide all aspects of your life. Then we went from the macro view (your place in society/community) and gradually sharpened our focus until we were looking at the micro level (relationships and daily self-focused activities). Now, we want to create a ring of protection around these macro- and micro- arenas of your life. We're looking at the substructure (finances and work) that exists to sustain and protect all these other values-driven aspects of your life. Hence, the work you will do for the remainder of this chapter will culminate in the creation of a Professional Development Strategy.

To reach that point, remember that you will be working through this strategy formulation model:

One more time, this section (Your Financial Fire Process) is stylized in workbook form so that you can use it to record the work that will culminate in your Professional Development Plan. But you may use whatever document makes you feel comfortable and helps you stay organized.

Let's do this!

Your Problem Statement

1. Describe your successes and failures with money and your profession. Do you consider yourself a good or bad manager of finances? Are you fulfilled in your career?

2. Consider your current financial situation. Mark your present level of satisfaction for each:

Income		Expense		Job	
Most satisfied	☐	Most satisfied	☐	Most satisfied	☐
Satisfied	☐	Satisfied	☐	Satisfied	☐
Least satisfied	☐	Least satisfied	☐	Least satisfied	☐

3. List any behaviors, patterns, or circumstances in your life that seem to be undermining your professional/financial development. What feels contradictory to your values as they relate to your employment and/or your management of finances?

4. Summarize your previous answers into a brief sentence or paragraph. Identify any barriers or obstacles to your professional development that you wish to overcome. This is your Financial Fire Problem Statement.

Your Vision Statement

1. It is now 5 years in the future. What have you accomplished in terms of your Financial Fires? What amazing transformation occurred in you these last 5 years?

2. Consider how you managed your time, talents, and resources over the last 5 years. In terms of your Financial Fires, describe any changes you would now make, in hindsight.

3. Summarize your previous answers into a brief sentence or paragraph. Consider how your vision of the future addresses your Financial Fires Problem

Statement. Identify anything that encourages you to leap out of bed each morning. This is your Financial Fires Vision Statement.

Your Mission Statement

1. Consider your professional satisfaction and financial health. What obvious or subtle changes are necessary within these arenas of your life? Describe anything that conflicts with your core values.

2. Briefly list a few actions or endeavors that would initiate these necessary changes.

3. Refer back to your Problem Statement and Vision Statement. What specific things must you do now to light and tend your Financial Fire?

4. Summarize your previous answers into a brief, action-oriented sentence or paragraph. This is your Financial Fire Mission Statement.

Your Values and Beliefs

A. Refer back to your Personal Definition Strategy under the Spiritual Fires section. Are there any values that are absent from that list that you now require to accomplish a Professional Development Strategy? If not, simply transfer those values in the spaces below.

B. Beliefs are your current perspectives, opinions, and conclusions based upon your cumulative knowledge and understanding. Refer back to your Personal Definition Strategy under the Spiritual Fires section. Are there any beliefs that are absent from that list that you now require to accomplish a Professional Development Strategy? If not, simply transfer those values in spaces below.

Goals and Objectives

This section of the Financial Fire Process is truly the moment when you can take your fifth lighter and light the torches that will protect the investments you have made, allowing all areas of your life to flourish in safety.

You now have an opportunity to contemplate which goals you wish to accomplish in the Financial Fire portion of F.I.R.E.S.

In this section, you will be using a model for goal-setting that involves identifying hurdles or challenges, figuring how you will measure your progress, and determining any timelines or deadlines for realizing these goals.

Now, turn the page and define your goals for lighting and tending your Financial Fire.

Set Your Goals

To set your goals, remember that you need to define your barriers, your index (way of measuring success), and your timeframe.

Financial

An example of a Financial goal is:

My goal is to overcome my credit card debt (barrier) by saving 15% of my paycheck each week (index: a metric and a measure), by the end of the month (timeframe).

Briefly write up to 3 goals within the model framework above and then transfer your answers to the next page. On the following page, complete the assignment by writing the 3 necessary steps required (i.e., objectives) to successfully accomplish each goal.

Goal #1

My goal is to: by: by the end of:

Goal #2

My goal is to: by: by the end of:

Goal #3

My goal is to: by: by the end of:

Chapter Six

Set Your Objectives

1. My goal is to   by   within

1.1. Objective   1.2. Objective   1.3. Objective

2. My goal is to   by   within

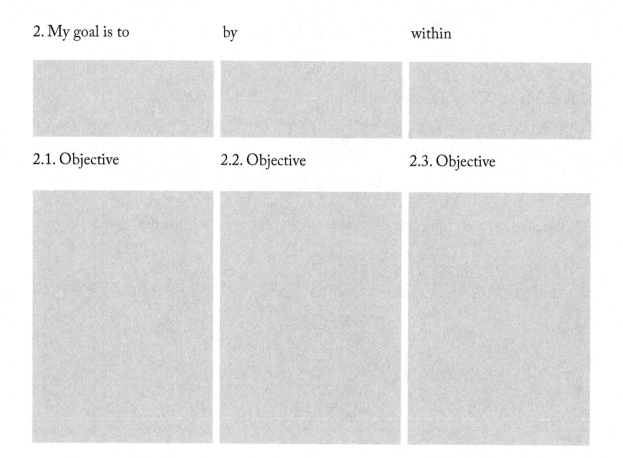

2.1. Objective   2.2. Objective   2.3. Objective

3. My goal is to   by   within

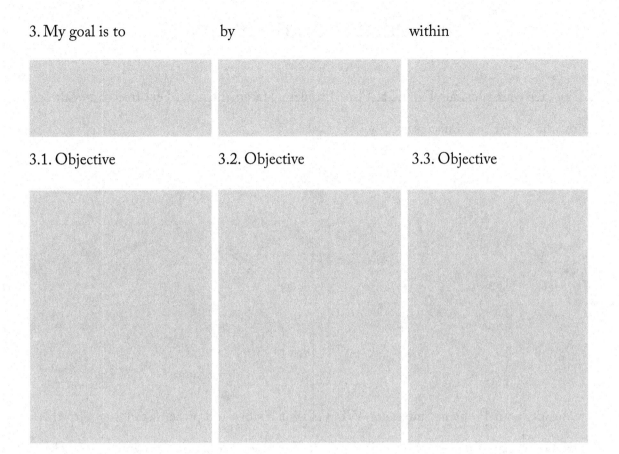

3.1. Objective   3.2. Objective   3.3. Objective

Your Situational Analysis

1. Transfer your previous Financial Fires Problem Statement here. Feel free to tweak or adjust the statement, if necessary.

2. Consider your Problem Statement. What is your history and present standing with this issue? Write a brief paragraph describing these successes and failures. Provide perspective, background, and insight on where you are coming from.

Chapter Six

Your Weaknesses and Strengths

List the 5 main strengths you have that can be used to light and tend your Financial Fire.

1.

2.

3.

4.

5.

F.I.R.E.S.

List the 5 main weaknesses you have that may present challenges as you light and tend your Financial Fire.

1.

2.

3.

4.

5.

Chapter Six

Your Boundaries

When formulating a strategy, there are sometimes boundaries on or limitations to the quality and quantity of alternatives you can feasibly implement.

In the space below, list or describe any resource constraints, prohibitions, concerns or guidelines that might limit your continued formulation of a strategy to light and tend your Financial Fires. This may include time, money, desire, motivation, strengths, weaknesses, opportunities and threats.

The Scenario Phase

Congratulations on progressing to Phase Three… the Scenario Phase! All of the Financial Fire work you completed up to this point is critically important. Your previous statements and activities will now guide you through brainstorming the possible alternatives and solutions to achieving your desired results.

Problems + Solutions
Goal One

My Financial Fires Problem Statement is:

1 . My goal is to   by   within

1.1. Objective   1.2. Objective   1.3. Objective

Brainstorm possible solutions to your Problem Statement or alternative ways to accomplish your goals here. Circle your best options after you have finished.

Problems + Solutions
Goal Two

My Financial Fires Problem Statement is:

2. My goal is to   by   within

2.1. Objective   2.2. Objective   2.3. Objective

Brainstorm possible solutions to your Problem Statement or alternative ways to accomplish your goals here. Circle your best options after you have finished.

Problems + Solutions
Goal Three

My Financial Fires Problem Statement is:

3. My goal is to   by   within

3.1. Objective   3.2. Objective   3.3. Objective

Brainstorm possible solutions to your Problem Statement or alternative ways to accomplish your goals here. Circle your best options after you have finished.

Think and Reason

Review the possible solutions and alternatives you circled over the last few pages. Why did you choose those circled items and not others to achieve your goals and objectives?

Accountability

How will you remain personally accountable to resolving your Financial Fires Problem Statement and to achieving each goal and objective?

How will you track progress and measure your results? What system of organization or other methodology will you use to collect data and manage improvements?

To ensure a successful completion of your goals and objectives, you will need feedback and focus. Choose an "Accountability Partner" to whom you will regularly communicate progress. This can be a relative, a friend, or another trusted person. We recommend someone (other than your spouse) who will keep your best interests in mind.

Accountability Partner: _____

Accountability Partner: _____

Enough talk...implement!

The following page is a summary sheet of the key statements, goals, and solutions necessary to accomplish your Professional Development Strategy. Tape a copy of this summary to your bathroom mirror, your refrigerator, or wherever else you need to be reminded of your personal commitment.

Return to this Internal Fires section in a few weeks after your strategy implementation, to re-evaluate your progress and success.

Enough talk... implement!

Professional Development Strategy

Problem Statement

Vision Statement

Mission Statement

Problem Solutions

F.I.R.E.S.

Strategy start date: _____

Strategy end date:_____

Accountability Partner:_____

Accountability Partner:_____

1. My goal is to   by   within

1.1. Objective   1.2. Objective   1.3. Objective

2. My goal is to   by   within

2.1. Objective   2.2. Objective   2.3. Objective

3. My goal is to   by   within

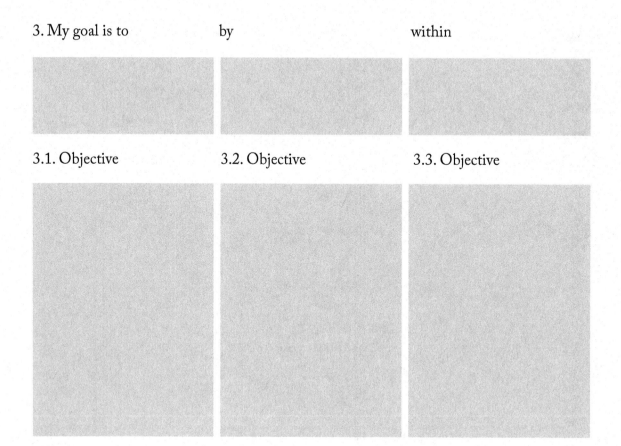

3.1. Objective   3.2. Objective   3.3. Objective

Chapter Six

Re-evaluation

1. Now that several weeks have passed since you implemented your Professional Development Strategy, briefly describe your success in resolving your Financial Fires Problem Statement. Are you celebrating each accomplishment?

2. Refer back to the Financial Fires Vision Statement you wrote describing your desired picture of the future. Is the "future" you are now experiencing anything like you expected back then? Why or why not?

3. What tweaks or changes must you make to your Professional Development Strategy? Are you on track to resolve your original Financial Fires Problem Statement and related goals? Is it time to repeat these process steps to resolve a new Financial Fires Problem Statement?

Financial Fire: Core Messages

Your Financial Fire is a profession and money management approach that creates a ring of protection around your balanced, values-driven life.

All too often, the demands of work and financial management burn out of control, consuming energy from areas of our lives that should be supported and sustained by a well-managed Financial Fire.

The biggest obstacle to lighting and tending a protective Financial Fire tends to originate in the mind. Mindsets like "work-spend-work-spend" and risk aversion can prevent you from moving forward in your life when it comes to work and finances.

Seven

A Life On Fire

The never-ending road to harnessing life's fires

It Made Sense On Paper

Have you ever heard the tale of the snake solution that went terribly, terribly wrong?

The story goes that in the days when India was a British colony, there was a cobra infestation in the city of Delhi. These venomous, hooded nightmares were rearing up everywhere, terrifying the population. So the British governor came up with what he thought was a perfectly straightforward solution.

Instead of sending government-appointed snake exterminators out into the city, he'd outsource the job to Delhi's denizens. He offered a bounty on cobra skins and made sure to set it high. The British Empire's pockets were deep and the governor wanted the problem resolved as efficiently as possible.

At first, the bounty worked well. Local people set out to slaughter the snakes *en masse* and claim their reward. But then, things took a turn.

Suddenly, a trickle of Delhi citizens realized they could turn a profit on this whole snake bounty thing. Because the governor had set the bounty so high, the reward for each snakeskin was much higher than the cost of breeding and raising a cobra.

So they started setting up cobra farms. Soon enough, thousands of snakes were being reared, killed, and traded in for bounties. The British Empire ended up making cobra propagation—rather than cobra elimination—richly profitable.

When the governor caught on to this, he called off the bounty, disappointing a large number of enterprising snake farmers. They released their unprofitable cobras into the city, making the infestation many times worse than it had been.

That's why, to this day, strategists talk about "the cobra effect", a phenomenon that occurs when the solution to a problem makes it much worse. This specific type of unintended consequence is only one way in which our "best laid plans" can turn against us.

Creating a strategy, a plan of action, or a solution is a powerful act. But having the commitment to continually refine that plan is more powerful by far. And that road to refinement never ends. It takes courage and good common sense to recognize when the bounty you set is inspiring your snake exterminators to become cobra farmers. It takes wisdom and commitment to your core values to make the necessary adjustments. (And you'd just better hope that after you make those necessary adjustments, your citizens don't start releasing their venomous charges into the city streets.)

One last time, let's revisit our fantasy of the five lighters. In this fantasy, you had the chance to change your relationship to fire, the raw power that resides in specific areas of your life. A destructive blaze that once engulfed your entire world was magically subdued and you were able to rest from your exhausting labor of constant fire fighting. The five lighters arrayed themselves before you, floating in mid-air. You picked up each one and intentionally lit five specific fires.

You used the first lighter to start a controlled burn of the clutter and tangled vegetation that had accumulated around your property. You began to harness your Spiritual Fire.

You used the second lighter to start a fire in a large brick oven in the courtyard. You began to harness your External Fire.

You used the third lighter to start a fire in the fireplace that warms your home.

You began to harness your Relational Fire.

You used the fourth lighter to light a lantern that illuminates your home. You began to harness your Internal Fire.

You used the fifth lighter to light the torches that surround your property and keep predatory animals away. You began to harness your Financial Fire.

Ultimately, you transformed yourself from a fire fighter to a fire tender. What a miracle! Fire was once a force that exhausted and overwhelmed you. It is now supplying spiritual clarity, social cooking fuel, interpersonal heat, personal illumination, and financial and professional security. You are standing in the middle of a terrifically productive, peaceful, and beautiful property—and it's all yours.

You have the power of fire on your side. But with power comes responsibility. How seriously will you now take your job as a fire tender?

The fact is that you'll never be completely inoculated from the threat of fires raging out of control. An errant spark can easily escape its confine of oven, hearth place, or torch, setting off blazes where they aren't wanted. Your long career as a fire fighter can always be reactivated if the situation calls for it.

Even the way in which you carefully, conscientiously tend your five fires can get you into trouble sometimes. "Best laid plans", right? When you're working within an entire system of fires, it's tricky to keep everything on track. Certain fires can burn out or burn out of control. Certain fires can begin consuming too much fuel, leaving inadequate supplies for the other blazes.

For example, what if you created a lofty Social Contribution Plan, but your Professional

Development Plan doesn't end up providing enough financing? Or your goals to spend more time with family and friends are derailed by your Personal Development Plan goals, which entail lengthy training sessions for running a marathon? Or what if after you've deployed your five strategies, you find that many of them don't actually help you to express your core values at all? What if they end up taking you further from becoming the person you want and need to become?

Snake exterminators can easily become snake farmers if the price of the bounty isn't quite right. Unintended consequences do occur. Plans are only ever perfect on paper. Taking your F.I.R.E.S. journey to the point of having completed all five components of your personal strategic plan is actually just a warm up. The real adventure—walking the road of refinement—is ahead of you.

That's what this final chapter is all about: taking a good, long look at the big picture of your strategies, and gathering up the motivation, inspiration, and commitment to continually refine them.

Five Fires: A Final Look

Before you take that long, hard look at your overall plan in action, let's take a little time to revisit what you learned about each fire.

Each of the five fires listed in my F.I.R.E.S. backronym is an aspect of your life that is packed with fuel. When we light these fuel sources and tend their fires intentionally, we reap the benefits of a balanced, on-purpose life. But when these five fires ignite without our governance and grow uncontrollably, we suffer from stress, fatigue, depression, and unproductive problem solving.

Spiritual Fire

Your Spiritual Fire is your system of core values and deepest beliefs. These are the principles that guide your actions and the convictions you hold to be true even when there is little or no evidence to support them.

It's all too easy to live on autopilot, failing to ever examine your core values and deepest beliefs. Nevertheless, your (examined or unexamined) matrix of beliefs and values propels your actions, and those actions lead to outcomes. In the end, those outcomes equal the sum total of your impact on the world.

When you choose to actively light and tend a well-managed Spiritual Fire, you experience a clearing away of the unnecessary. You have enhanced clarity and creativity around what is essential. Spiritual Fire is, above all else, refining and regenerating in nature.

Spiritual Fire kick-starts the F.I.R.E.S. because clarity around your core values and deepest beliefs will help you make more meaningful choices in the other areas of your life.

External Fire

Your External Fire is whatever you do to make a contribution to community at any scale. It's about taking that clarity you developed around your core values and deepest beliefs and doing something about it, starting with the world outside your door.

When you choose to actively light and tend a well-managed External Fire, you create virtuous cycles of connectedness and community. When you invest in community, you can draw upon its resources when you need them. External Fire is ultimately about abundance.

External Fire follows Spiritual Fire because investing into, and being able to draw from, community will put the rest of your needs into perspective. Cultivating true abundance in your life by serving community makes your self-focused, short-range, and immediate needs easier to define and fulfill. When your External Fire is lit and preparing that communal food, you are operating from a baseline of abundance.

Relational Fire

Your Relational Fire is the result of your investment into relationships with family, friends, and fellows. It continues the theme of expressing your core values and deepest beliefs, but at a more intimate, day-to-day scale than you do with External Fire.

When you choose to actively light and tend a well-managed Relational Fire, you access the type of nurturance you need in order to be the person you want to be. If External Fire is about giving abundantly in order to access the abundance you need, Relational Fire is about nurturing intentionally in order to access the nurturance you need. In both, you get what you give.

Both the fuel of kindness it feeds on and the clearly marked boundaries it burns within define Relational Fire. This fire needs intentional fuel: acts of calm attentiveness, support, and respect. It also needs to burn in a fireplace, rather than raging throughout the whole home. This "fireplace" is created by boundaries, the guidelines we set around how we are to be treated, and what consequences will result if these guidelines are ignored. Without them, a fire meant to warm our home becomes a force consuming everything precious to us, including our sense of self as well as our ability to express core values.

Internal Fire

Your Internal Fire is the result of where you invest your self-focused, free time and energy; it's about what you do for you. Internal Fire shines a light on the path you walk every day, providing immediate direction. It gives you a sense of what to do in the small moments that end up meaning everything.

When you choose to actively light and tend a well-managed Internal Fire, you ensure that the things you do for you are bringing you closer to becoming the person you want to become. How you spend your personal time will end up determining the trajectory of your personal development.

The "stuff" of your Internal Fire is found in the way you manage your holistic health, the hobbies you pursue, and the hopes you hold regarding personal goals and dreams. These "Three H's" are starting points for considering how you invest your free, self-focused time and energy. They are fairly simple and entirely concrete arenas of attention and time investment that happen to be deep drivers of change.

Financial Fire

Your Financial Fire is a profession and money management approach that creates a ring of protection around your balanced, values-driven life. It surrounds and supports everything else you have invested into, making all the good things in your life possible—and, ultimately, sustainable.

All too often, the demands of work and financial management burn out of control, consuming energy from areas of our lives that should be supported and sustained by a well managed Financial Fire. But metrics like hours spent at work or zeros on a paycheck are meaningless in the context of an unbalanced, joyless life. Professional and financial success only gain meaning if they sustain a life well lived.

The biggest obstacle to lighting and tending a protective Financial Fire tends to originate in the mind. Mindsets like "work-spend-work-spend" and risk aversion can prevent you from moving ahead when it comes to work and finances. To become a Master of Living, who, in the words of Lawrence Pearsall Jacks "simply pursues his vision of excellence through whatever he is doing, and leaves others to determine whether he is working or playing," you must tackle the mindsets that hold you back.

Mastery of all five fires results in a balanced, values-driven life in which you will continuously move towards becoming the person you dream of becoming. The five plans within your F.I.R.E.S. personal strategic plan should fit together synergistically, supporting each other in a balanced whole. But it's not easy to achieve and maintain this balance, as you'll surely see once you have executed your five strategies and monitored your progress for a little while. Goals will conflict. Strategies will backfire. That's why the motivation to continually refine them is a necessity.

Strategies for maintaining motivation

The road to refinement is long—life-long, in fact. Don't lose heart if you sometimes feel like your "best laid plans" have resulted in little more than blowback and unintended consequences. Any strategist worth their weight knows that revision is the key to eventual success. But to make those refinements, you need strategies for maintaining your motivation. Here are a few to try on for size.

Remember WHY

Implementing a multi-faceted personal strategic plan is like building an intricate cathedral, an awe-inspiring monument that takes a tremendous amount of labor and materials.

In the middle ages, such cathedrals took decades or even centuries to build. The process often began with a fundraising effort that involved taking holy relics on a world tour. Those tours had to be lucrative because they ended up bankrolling massive teams of laborers, including quarrymen, plasterers, mortar-makers, stone-cutters, and masons. Cathedrals that, to this day, hold the power to take a person's breath away represent tremendous amounts of hard work and coordinated resources.

But every cathedral begins with the laying of a single stone, its cornerstone. In masonry foundations, the cornerstone was significant because every other stone would be set in reference to it. The position of the cathedral could be traced back to this single, unassuming stone.

The first stone you are setting in the construction of your cathedral is your Why. The core values you articulated in Spiritual Fire are always there as a reference and a reminder. Your Spiritual Fire is a simple, ever-present clue as to the positioning of the other complex and interrelated components of your F.I.R.E.S. plan.

Cathedrals are designed to inspire awe, short-circuit your thinking, and instill the feeling of being part of something larger than yourself. As you implement and hone your strategies, you will be creating a life that defies simplistic analysis. There is strength and also liability in this. Manage the risk by remembering your cornerstone and revisiting it whenever necessary.

Everything complex and grand that you build began with the laying of a single, humble stone. Refer back to it whenever you need to regain your sense of clarity.

Emphasize "moving towards"

If you ever find you need a little extra wind in your sails on your journey, it helps to frame your mission as one of "moving towards" rather than "moving away from". It's often more motivating to remember the positive outcomes you wish to experience, rather than to fixate on the negative situations you wish to escape.

For example, if one of your goals is to lose thirty pounds, you could articulate your rationale for that goal in a number of ways. You could say, "I want to lose thirty pounds because I would feel more able, confident, and energetic." Or you could say, "I want to lose thirty pounds because I'm so limited in what I can do and I feel ashamed of my appearance."

The first way emphasizes moving towards a desired outcome. The second emphasizes moving away from a negative situation.

Problem-solving is an extraordinary capability of human beings. Often, we are motivated to act only when we really connect with our "pain points". (And hey—each of your five planning processes began with the articulation of problems you wanted to solve.) But many schools of thought, including positive psychology and Appreciative Inquiry, assert that sustaining your motivation to manage change is easier when you focus on the positive.

When you feel your enthusiasm for executing and trouble-shooting your strategies is flagging, just remember all that you have to gain. It can give you the boost you need to stay in the game.

Nurture a growth mindset

What's your relationship with failure like? Is it a dysfunctional, tear-your-hair-out, deflating dynamic, or a happy, peaceful partnership that supports your success?

What? You didn't realize failure could become your best friend? If you had what the psychologist Carole Dweck calls a "growth mindset", you would know that was the case.

Dweck has found that people who believe they can improve generally do. People who see their failure as a necessary step on the way to success have a "growth mindset". They believe that abilities can be developed, and failure is an aspect of that development. On the other hand, people who believe that their capabilities (e.g., intelligence) are innate or fixed traits (i.e., they were either born with these gifts or not), tend to be devastated by failure. And these folks consequently don't grow or improve.

If you fail to reach a goal or an aspect of your F.I.R.E.S. plan misfires or backfires, will it derail and demotivate you? Or will you believe in your ability to improve your plan and, by extension, yourself. Incredibly, this belief has real, scientifically verified power to propel you towards eventual success. Inventor Thomas A. Edison once remarked, "Our greatest weakness lies in giving up. The most certain way to succeed is always to try just one more time."

When you struggle, remind yourself, "I—along with every other person on this planet— have the ability to grow and improve. Failure is my friend."

Chapter Seven

A life on fire

You, my friend, could have a life on fire.

Not consumed by the conflagrations of stress, confusion, and malaise, but on fire. As in: lit up, fired up, roaring away, and on purpose. Not a life that forces you to slave away as a fire fighter, but one that invests in you the responsibilities and rewards of the fire tender.

Mastery of the Spiritual, External, Relational, Internal, and Financial aspects of your life is a life-long process. It requires commitment to your core values and motivation to sustain change management. It requires the ability to make adaptations, with the understanding that failure is your friend, your Why is worth it, and you're always moving towards what you desire.

Take it from this song-writing strategy geek and recovering corporate drone: you're going somewhere you want to be. Choose balance over busy-ness, purpose over pointlessness, and growth over giving up, and you'll never regret it.

I've done my best to teach you the tools that I acquired while working with some of the most awesomely successful companies on the planet. I know how well they work for coordinating the resources of massively profitable corporations. And I know how well they work for coordinating the resources of a richly promising human life.

You just have to invest time and effort into learning to use these tools. The more you invest, the more you will reap the rewards of life mastery.

The life you want to lead and the person you want to become are available to you, stored up inside of you as pure potential. You have all the fuel you need to live a life on fire.

Go ahead; burn brightly.

Your F.I.R.E.S. Refinement Workbook

Your F.I.R.E.S. Refinement Process

Maybe it's been a long while since you created and launched your F.I.R.E.S. personal strategic plan, involving strategies for lighting and tending your Spiritual, External, Relational, Internal, and Financial Fires. Maybe it's been a relatively short time; say, a few months. Maybe you're revisiting this section for the millionth time. Maybe you feel it's time, once again, to take stock of the fires you've been tending, and the life you've been building.

If this is your first time working your way through this section of the book, mark this page. You should return to it as often as you need to over the weeks, months, and years to come. This is the place where you can assess your F.I.R.E.S. strategy as a whole, evaluating how well your five plans cohere, and whether you're on track to expressing your core values in all areas of your life.

In creating your F.I.R.E.S. personal strategic plan, you took quite the journey. Let's review all the major milestones:

Financial: You want and need professional/financial security and success

Internal: You want and need a holistically healthy day to day existence

Relational: You want and need good relationships with friends and family

External: You want and need to make social/community contributions

Spiritual: You want and need, above all else, to live out your core values

Of course, you took this journey in the reverse order, starting with your Personal Definition Strategy, which informed every step that followed it. From defining core values, you moved towards a macro-level expression of these values with your Social Contribution Strategy. Then, you sharpened your focus and narrowed your scope to create your Relationship and Personal Development Strategies. Finally, you created a ring of protection around these parts of your balanced life with a Professional Development Strategy.

So…how has life been since you made these plans? What's been working well together? What not so much? How is the overall "system" of your five fires functioning? Any errant sparks, out of control blazes, or accidentally extinguished fires?

It's time to take stock of your progress and determine whether any of your goals or strategies require adjustments. To facilitate this, we'll be following the same model you used to create your five strategies. One more time, that model looked like:

One more time, this section (Your F.I.R.E.S. Refinement Process) is stylized like a workbook so that you can use it to record the work that will culminate in your F.I.R.E.S. Refinement Plan. But since you should revisit this section whenever you need to make adjustments to your goals or strategies, it might make sense to start a separate folder or document. You may end up using a lot of paper as you continually refine your plans!

Your Problem Statement

1. Describe the best—most wonderful, positive, successful, or powerful—outcomes that you can directly link to actions you took in accordance with your F.I.R.E.S. strategic plans.

2. Describe any unintended negative consequences that you can directly link to actions you took in accordance with your F.I.R.E.S. strategic plans.

Income		Expense		Job	
Most satisfied	☐	Most satisfied	☐	Most satisfied	☐
Satisfied	☐	Satisfied	☐	Satisfied	☐
Least satisfied	☐	Least satisfied	☐	Least satisfied	☐

3. List any elements within any of your five plans that conflict with or undermine one another. List any elements within any of your five plans that conflict with or undermine your core values.

4. Summarize your previous answers into a brief sentence or paragraph. Identify any barriers or obstacles to the values-driven life you imagined for yourself at the start of your F.I.R.E.S. journey. This is your F.I.R.E.S. Refinement Problem Statement.

Your Vision Statement

1. It is now 5 years in the future. What are the most significant things you have accomplished in terms of your F.I.R.E.S. personal strategic plan? What amazing transformation has occurred in you these last 5 years?

2. Consider how you managed your time, talents, and resources to balance the demands of your Spiritual, External, Relational, Internal, and Financial Fires over the last 5 years. Describe, in hindsight, any changes you would now make.

3. Summarize your previous answers into a brief sentence or paragraph. Consider how your vision of the future addresses your F.I.R.E.S. Refinement Problem Statement. Identify anything that encourages you to leap out of bed each morning. This is your F.I.R.E.S. Refinement Vision Statement.

Chapter Seven

Your Mission Statement

1. Consider your level of satisfaction in the outcomes your F.I.R.E.S. personal strategic plan has generated. What obvious or subtle changes are still necessary within the Spiritual, External, Relational, Internal, and Financial areas of your life? Describe anything that conflicts with your core values.

2. Briefly list a few actions or endeavors that would initiate these necessary changes.

3. Refer back to your Problem Statement and Vision Statement. What specific things must you do now to refine your F.I.R.E.S. personal strategic plan?

4. Summarize your previous answers into a brief, action-oriented sentence or paragraph. This is your F.I.R.E.S. Refinement Mission Statement.

Your Values and Beliefs

A. Refer back to your Personal Definition Strategy under the Spiritual Fires section. Are there any values that are absent from that list that you now realize are important to you? If not, simply transfer those values in the spaces below.

B. Beliefs are your current perspectives, opinions, and conclusions based upon your cumulative knowledge and understanding. Refer back to your Personal Definition Strategy under the Spiritual Fires section. Are there any beliefs that are absent from that list that you now realize are important to you? If not, simply transfer those values in spaces below.

Goals and Objectives

This section of the F.I.R.E.S. Refinement Process is the moment when you can take the big picture perspective of how your F.I.R.E.S. personal strategic plan functions overall and refine it accordingly.

You now have an opportunity to contemplate which goals you wish to adjust, add, or remove from any of your five F.I.R.E.S. plans.

In this section, you will be using a model for goal-setting that involves identifying hurdles or challenges, figuring how you will measure your progress, and determining any timelines or deadlines for realizing these goals.

Now, turn the page and refine and redefine your goals.

Reset Your Goals

To reset your goals, remember that you need to define your barriers, your index (way of measuring success), and your timeframe.

Briefly write up to 3 revised or reset goals within the model framework above and then

transfer your answers to the next page. On the following page, complete the assignment by

writing the 3 necessary steps required (i.e., objectives) to successfully accomplish each goal.

Goal #1

My goal is to: by: by the end of:

Goal #2

My goal is to: by: by the end of:

Goal #3

My goal is to: by: by the end of:

Reset Your Objectives

1. My goal is to   by   within

1.1. Objective   1.2. Objective   1.3. Objective

2. My goal is to   by   within

2.1. Objective   2.2. Objective   2.3. Objective

3. My goal is to   by   within

3.1. Objective   3.2. Objective   3.3. Objective

Your Situational Analysis

1. Transfer your previous F.I.R.E.S. Refinement Problem Statement here. Feel free to tweak or adjust the statement, if necessary.

2. Consider your Problem Statement. What is your history and present standing with this issue? Write a brief paragraph describing these successes and failures. Provide perspective, background, and insight on where you are coming from.

Your Weaknesses and Strengths

List the 5 main strengths you have that can be used to refine your F.I.R.E.S. personal strategic plan.

1.

2.

3.

4.

5.

List the 5 main weaknesses you have that may present challenges as you refine your F.I.R.E.S. personal strategic plan.

1.

2.

3.

4.

5.

Your Boundaries

When formulating a strategy, there are sometimes boundaries on or limitations to the quality and quantity of alternatives you can feasibly implement.

In the space below, list or describe any resource constraints, prohibitions, concerns or guidelines that might limit your continued formulation of a strategy to light and tend your overall F.I.R.E.S. personal strategic plan. This may include time, money, desire, motivation, strengths, weaknesses, opportunities and threats.

The Scenario Phase

Congratulations on progressing to Phase Three… the Scenario Phase! All of the F.I.R.E.S. Refinement work you completed up to this point is critically important. Your previous statements and activities will now guide you through brainstorming the possible alternatives and solutions to achieving your desired results.

Problems + Solutions
Goal One

My Financial Fires Problem Statement is:

1 . My goal is to   by   within

1.1. Objective   1.2. Objective   1.3. Objective

Brainstorm possible solutions to your Problem Statement or alternative ways to accomplish your goals here. Circle your best options after you have finished.

Problems + Solutions
Goal Two

My Financial Fires Problem Statement is:

2. My goal is to   by   within

2.1. Objective   2.2. Objective   2.3. Objective

Brainstorm possible solutions to your Problem Statement or alternative ways to accomplish your goals here. Circle your best options after you have finished.

Chapter Seven

Problems + Solutions
Goal Three

My Financial Fires Problem Statement is:

3. My goal is to   by   within

3.1. Objective   3.2. Objective   3.3. Objective

Brainstorm possible solutions to your Problem Statement or alternative ways to accomplish your goals here. Circle your best options after you have finished.

Think and Reason

Review the possible solutions and alternatives you circled over the last few pages. Why did you choose those circled items and not others to achieve your goals and objectives?

Accountability

How will you remain personally accountable to resolving your F.I.R.E.S. Refinement Problem Statement and to achieving each goal and objective?

How will you track progress and measure your results? What system of organization or other methodology will you use to collect data and manage improvements?

To ensure a successful completion of your goals and objectives, you will need feedback and focus. Choose an "Accountability Partner" to whom you will regularly communicate progress. This can be a relative, a friend, or another trusted person. We recommend someone (other than your spouse) who will keep your best interests in mind.

Accountability Partner: _____

Accountability Partner: _____

Enough talk…implement!

The following page is a summary sheet of the key statements, goals, and solutions necessary to accomplish your F.I.R.E.S. Refinement Strategy. Tape a copy of this summary to your bathroom mirror, your refrigerator, or wherever else you need to be reminded of your personal commitment.

Return to this F.I.R.E.S. Refinement section in a few weeks after your strategy implementation, to re-evaluate your progress and success.

Enough talk… implement!

F.I.R.E.S. Refinement Strategy

Problem Statement

Vision Statement

Mission Statement

Problem Solutions

F.I.R.E.S.

Strategy start date: _____

Strategy end date:_____

Accountability Partner:_____

Accountability Partner:_____

1. My goal is to   by   within

1.1. Objective   1.2. Objective   1.3. Objective

2. My goal is to   by   within

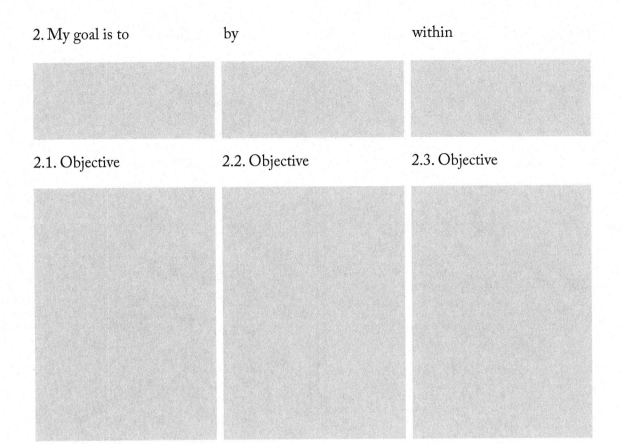

2.1. Objective   2.2. Objective   2.3. Objective

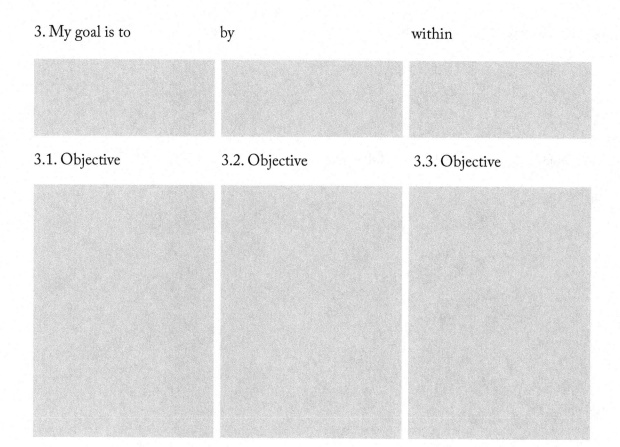

3. My goal is to   by   within

3.1. Objective   3.2. Objective   3.3. Objective

Re-evaluation

1. Now that several weeks have passed since you implemented your F.I.R.E.S. Refinement Strategy, briefly describe your success in resolving your F.I.R.E.S. Refinement Problem Statement. Are you celebrating each accomplishment?

2. Refer back to the F.I.R.E.S. Refinement Vision Statement you wrote describing your desired picture of the future. Is the "future" you are now experiencing anything like you expected back then? Why or why not?

3. What tweaks or changes must you make to your F.I.R.E.S. Refinement Strategy? Are you on track to resolve your original F.I.R.E.S. Refinement Problem Statement and related goals? Is it time to repeat these process steps to resolve a new F.I.R.E.S. Refinement Problem Statement?

Notes

Chapter Two

Start with Why: How Great Leaders Inspire Everyone to Take Action by Simon Sinek. Portfolio, 2011.

Chapter Three

Community and Growth by Jean Vanier. Paulist Press, 2002.

Loneliness: Human Nature and the Need for Social Connection by John T. Cacioppo. WW Norton, 2009.

Chapter Four

Why Marriages Succeed or Fail: What You Can Learn from the Breakthrough Research to Make Your Marriage Last by John Gottman and Nan Silver. Simon & Schuster, 1994.

The Science of Happily Ever After: What Really Matters in the Quest for Enduring Love by Ty Tashiro. Harlequin, 2014.

Boundaries: When to Say Yes, How to Say No to Take Control of Your Life by Dr. Henry Cloud. Zondervan, 2002.

Chapter Five

The Power of Habit: Why We Do What We Do in Life and Business by Charles Duhigg. Random House Trade Paperbacks, 2014.

"Benefiting from creative activity: The positive relationships between creative activity, recovery experiences, and performance-related outcomes," by Kevin J. Eschleman, Jamie Madsen, Gene Alarcon, and Alex Barelka, Journal of Occupational and Organizational Psychology, 17 April 2014.

The 7 Habits of Highly Effective People: The 25th Anniversary Edition by Stephen Covey. Simon & Schuster, 2014.

Chapter Six

Education Through Recreation by Lawrence Pearsall Jacks. Harper & Brothers, 1932.

"Job Satisfaction: 2016 Edition: Tightening Labor Market Means More Opportunity, More Satisfaction," by The Conference Board, July 2016. www.conference-board.org/publications/publicationdetail.cfm?publicationid=7250&centerId=4

"2016 American Credit Card Debt Study" by Erin Il Issa, Nerdwallet. www.nerdwallet.com/blog/average-credit-card-debt-household

"The relationship between personal unsecured debt and mental and physical health: a systematic review and meta-analysis," by T. Richardson, P. Elliott, and R. Roberts. Clinical Psychology Review, December 2013.

Rich Dad, Poor Dad: What The Rich Teach Their Kids About Money That the Poor and Middle Class Do Not! by Robert Kiyosaki. Market Paperback, 2011.

"Ideal Lifestyle Costing" by Tim Ferriss, tim.blog/lifestyle-costing

The Overworked American: The Unexpected Decline Of Leisure by Juliet Schor. Basic Books, 1993.

Chapter Seven

Mindset: The New Psychology of Success by Carol S. Dweck. Ballantine Books, 2007.

Author Biography

Daniel L. Purdy, Sr. is an executive coach and management consultant with over 20 years of experience working in Fortune 500s, mid-size companies, and start-ups. He was previously employed by global giants such as: AECOM; British Petroleum (BP); Hewlett-Packard (HP); Agilent Technologies; and Freeport-McMoran Copper & Gold. He has also owned and operated small businesses since 2005.

Mr. Purdy is the Founder and President of Daring Business Strategies, Inc., the parent corporation of both Kaizen Assembly and his Express Employment Professionals franchise, a full-service staffing and recruiting firm based in Abbotsford, British Columbia. Mr. Purdy purchased Kaizen Assembly in 2017 and serves as both President and Senior LEAN Consultant.

Mr. Purdy presently delivers both strategic and tactical project-based management consulting services to manufacturers and various service providers in the U.S. and Canada. He is proficient in strategic planning, continuous process improvement, LEAN training and implementation, team coaching, mentoring and development, PSCM systems/process, supplier sourcing and qualification, competitive bidding, subcontract negotiations, materials management, and detailed data analysis.

- MBA, Business Management - Information Technology, Colorado State University, 1999
- BBA, Business Administration - International Business, Andrews University, 1995
- Certified Professional in Supply Management (CPSM), Institute of Supply Management, 2011 – 2017
- Lean Six Sigma Black Belt (LSSBB), Purdue University, 2011

More About Daniel

Daring Business Strategies, Inc. is a multi-national corporation based in Lynden, Washington USA on the border with British Columbia, Canada. Through our family of Bible-based companies and brands, we seek to maintain an impressive bench of executive/management consultants, coaches, trainers, LEAN experts, and LEAN practitioners. Our associates bring decades of professional experience in a variety of manufacturing and/or service environments.

Daring Business Strategies, Inc. (www.daring.biz) is the multi-national parent corporation of each management consulting firm and brand. Its primary services include Strategic Planning, Business Planning, Executive Coaching and Mentoring. Established in June 2005, it remains privately held by Daniel L. Purdy, Sr.

Kaizen Assembly, LLC (www.kaizenassembly.com) is a premier LEAN consulting, training, and implementation firm. The company was wholly acquired by Mr. Purdy in January 2017. Manufacturing and Service clients achieve measurable performance results in: lead time reductions; productivity improvements; floor space optimization; activity travel distance reduction; greater inventory alignment; cost synergies; and better product/service quality.

Express Employment Professionals (www.expresspros.com) is an award-winning, full-service staffing and recruiting firm, with over 770 locations throughout the U.S., Canada, and South Africa. Mr. Purdy owns the franchise territory covering Abbotsford, Chilliwack, Mission, Maple Ridge and Pitt Meadows, British Columbia.

F.I.R.E.S.™ and Fighting Life's Fires™ (www.FIRES.org) is a personal strategic planning system designed by Mr. Purdy to Reset, Redefine, and Realign™ unproductive paradigms with proven methods of success. The five module workbook methodology helps businesses, individuals, and small groups learn to balance their Financial, Internal, Relational, External, and Spiritual (F.I.R.E.S.™) fires.

CPSIA information can be obtained
at www.ICGtesting.com
Printed in the USA
FSOW04n1041301117
41848FS